To Nancy,

WHAT'S FOR BREAKFAST?

Mary Anne Bauer

What a special friend you are! With love and all my good wishes for good mornings! ♡ Mary Anne Bauer

A Nitty Gritty® Cookbook

© 1988, Bristol Publishing Enterprises, Inc., P.O. Box 1737, San Leandro, California 94577. World rights reserved.

Printed in the United States of America.

ISBN 0-911954-90-2

Production Consultant:
   Vicki L. Crampton
Photographer: Kathryn Opp
Food Stylist:
   Carolyn Schirmacher Gerould and
      Barbara Brooks
Illustrator: Carol Webb Atherly

For their cooperation in sharing props and locations for use in photographs, we extend special thanks to The Country Willow, Plat du Jour and Virginia Jacobs. Tupperware courtesy of Janet Bunyard.

Table of Contents

This book is dedicated to my family and friends for their constant love, encouragement and support. I'm sure they're delighted that breakfast is over and it's time for lunch!

Special thanks to Miki Van Housten, whose culinary skills coupled with scientific flair helped to develop many of the breakfast cookies and bars, and to Vicki Ford, who was ever ready with love, support and recipes. And thanks to the people who shared ideas as well as tasting and testing: Jack Kennedy, S.J., Bill Zelkie, S.J., Marsha and Chuck Floberg, Patty Brandt, Jan Hyneman, Joanel Zinman, Kathy Brown, Ron Holmgren, Pat Pfenning, and I.H. Stone.

Introduction

When Pat Collins of Bristol Publishing asked me if I'd be interested in writing a breakfast book, I was delighted. Not just because I love to write, love to cook and most of all love to share ideas, but because breakfast has always been an important part of the day for me. I am a true morning person. I love to get up early and greet that fresh new day, that new beginning.

When people learned about my project, many said, "I love breakfast, but I just don't have time." So there are dozens of ideas for people on the run.

Others said, "Oh, I love breakfast, but only if I can linger over it." So there are ideas for leisurely weekend breakfasts to be savored with family or friends.

Some said, "I hope you won't forget the old favorites." So you will find familiar recipes, many with ideas for saving time and adding variations.

And some said, "I never eat breakfast." And for those reluctant breakfast eaters I have plenty of tempting ideas.

I love any excuse to celebrate, and include a chapter on special occasion and holiday breakfasts: everything from birthdays to fuss-free Christmas mornings, first day of school for relieved moms and Valentine's Day menus.

So, *What's for Breakfast?* Fast, delicious and frequently unique morning meals for everybody and every occasion!

Breakfast Can Be Fun

Try some of these to spark up tired morning appetites. They'll head off to school or work with a nutritious start to the day and a smile.

- Fill a honeydew melon wedge with ham cubes and top with cinnamon apple yogurt.
- Fill a small half melon with a scoop of frozen yogurt.
- Fill a small half melon with cottage cheese and top with granola cereal or Grape-Nuts, or raisins, or dried fruit or nuts.
- Spread a frozen waffle with peanut butter and honey.
- Make a waffle sandwich with bacon and egg or fruit and sour cream or yogurt filling.
- Toast a frozen waffle, top with fruit yogurt and sprinkle with nuts, Grape-Nuts, coconut or granola.
- Spread toast or a waffle with chunky peanut butter, top with sliced bananas and sprinkle with coconut.
- Whip apple butter with cottage cheese and sprinkle with granola and raisins.

- Spread toast with peanut butter, add a layer of grated carrots and top with granola.

- Make breakfast salads served with bowls of toppings.

- Serve fruit yogurt sprinkled with Grape-Nuts or granola.

- Stir a tablespoon of peanut butter into hot oatmeal.

- Top hot or cold cereal with applesauce, sprinkle with cinnamon and pour milk over all.

- Top cereal with fresh fruit and sprinkle with coconut.

- Make a face out of raisins, fruit and nuts on peanut butter toast or toast spread with cream cheese and honey. Make coconut hair.

- Create a face made of assorted fruits on a bowl of cooked cereal to delight a preschooler.

- Fill a small half melon with cereal. Pour milk over cereal and enjoy both cereal and "bowl."

- Add a little honey and a drop of vanilla or almond extract to warm milk for a cold morning treat or to use on cereal.

- Make a breakfast "soda" by adding a scoop of frozen yogurt to a glass of juice. Add some club soda for "fizz."

- Spread peanut butter on slices of apple and sprinkle with raisins.

- How about a breakfast parfait? Layer cottage cheese and several fruits in a stemmed clear glass bowl. Beautiful! Try strawberries, grapes, blueberries, raspberries, kiwi. Then top with a tablespoon of raisin granola.

- Or a banana split? Slice a banana into three slices and arrange on the plate. Top with cinnamon-spiced cottage cheese or yogurt mixed with strawberries, or kiwi or blueberries.

- Rice cakes with topping. Try tuna salad . . . egg salad . . . cottage cheese and fruit . . . peanut butter and honey . . . peanut butter and banana . . . peanut butter and applesauce . . . mozzarella cheese melted . . . cottage cheese and seasonings and minced veggies.

- Fill an ice cream cone with chunky applesauce mixed with granola. Top with vanilla yogurt and sprinkle with cinnamon-sugar or nuts.

- Serve scrambled eggs in half of a pita bread.

- Serve Yogurt Popsicles (page 6) and granola.

It Doesn't Have To Look Like Breakfast

Teachers say they can pick out the child who has not had breakfast. He's usually tired by 10:00 AM. Even the reluctant breakfast eater will look forward to these unusual and quick treats.

Tip: Sometimes people who say they can't eat breakfast tend to snack late at night. Try to cut down on late night snacking and you may have more of a morning appetite.

Breakfast treats:

- cottage cheese dip for vegetables and whole wheat crackers
- peanuts and raisins and granola
- vegetable-hamburger soup and crackers

- **Yogurt Popsicles**

    1 qt. plain yogurt
    1 can (6 ozs.) orange juice concentrate
    ⅓ cup honey
    2 tsp. vanilla

    In a medium bowl, beat yogurt, thawed concentrate, honey and vanilla, blending well. Pour into small paper cups. Stand a plastic spoon in each cup for a handle. Freeze. To serve, peel away paper cup.

- cheddar cheese sticks, crackers and orange wedges

- **Broiled Apple and Cheese Sandwich**

    Toast bread. Add 1 slice of Swiss or Jack cheese. Arrange slices of apple or pear on cheese. Sprinkle with cinnamon and sugar. Broil until lightly golden and cheese is melted.

- tomato slices seasoned with basil, salt and pepper, topped with Parmesan cheese and broiled

- cold sliced meat loaf, apple slices and bread sticks

- meat loaf sandwich with tomato slices, lettuce and sprouts, served with a glass of milk
- cottage cheese mixed with grated carrot and raisins **or** mixed with green pepper, carrots and chopped tomato
- taco salad with all the fixings
- toasted cheese sandwich and a glass of fruit or tomato juice
- mug of canned tomato soup made with milk, whole wheat crackers and an apple
- onion soup with grated Parmesan cheese and toasted French bread
- custard and fruit and a mug of cocoa
- open-faced peanut butter sandwich topped with orange slices and a glass of milk
- leftover roast beef or ham sandwich on whole wheat bread
- deviled eggs, a piece of fruit and whole wheat crackers
- leftover chicken or turkey, an apple and a muffin

- taco with lettuce, tomatoes, meat and grated cheese — even olives
- rice pudding, or bread pudding, with raisins
- leftover macaroni and cheese with a glass of juice
- cottage cheese and fruit salad with a roll
- cottage cheese mixed with fruit, fresh, dried or canned
- leftover casserole, spaghetti, stew, or soup and whole wheat crackers
- lettuce salad with cheese, meat or eggs served with whole wheat toast
- leftover baked potato reheated with cheese
- baked apple filled with raisins, nuts, cinnamon and topped with honey-sweetened yogurt
- cottage cheese with unsweetened applesauce, topped with a sprinkling of Grape-Nuts or granola
- cream cheese mixed with chutney, served on a bagel or on a turkey sandwich

- apple filled with cranberry sauce, baked 20 minutes at 400°, a glass of milk and a roll
- peanut butter cookie sandwiches with cream cheese filling and a glass of orange juice
- oatmeal cookie sandwiches with honey-cream cheese filling and a glass of orange juice
- a thin slice of low fat or turkey bologna or ham, fried to form a cup, filled with scrambled eggs
- toast cups filled with scrambled eggs mixed with chopped ham and cheese
- Canadian bacon spread with marmalade, served with hot biscuits
- hot gingerbread topped with sweetened cream cheese and served with fruit
- mini-kabobs of small pieces of fruit on toothpicks or skewers
- **English muffin pizza:** top toasted English muffin halves with a tablespoon of pizza sauce and shredded Jack or mozzarella or Parmesan cheese
- sliced tomato on an English muffin half topped with a slice of cheddar or Jack cheese, broiled

- deviled eggs, sliced orange wheels and a roll

- a summer fruit sundae: a melon half filled with strawberries, blueberries or mixed cup-up fruit, topped with a dollop of honey-sweetened yogurt

- **Peanut Butter Surprise Sandwiches**

4 slices whole wheat bread	2 tbs. applesauce
butter or margarine	2 tbs. shredded apple
½ cup chunky peanut butter	lettuce (optional)

  Spread bread lightly with butter or margarine. In a small bowl, mix peanut butter and applesauce until well blended. Stir in apple. Spread 2 slices of bread with filling. Top with lettuce if desired and second slice of bread. Serves 2. Serve with milk and orange slices.

- other peanut butter sandwich additions:

banana slices	orange slices and coconut
apple sliced or chopped	applesauce
apple butter	honey and cinnamon
marmalade	chopped raisins

Breakfast On The Run

The car pool is waiting and you're late! But there is still time for a quick, tasty and nutritious start to the day. Here are some grab-and-run ideas for busy mornings.

- a couple of hard cooked eggs, several cherry tomatoes, and breadsticks
- apple or pear, sticks of cheddar cheese and a few almonds or peanuts
- cream cheese and raisins on a bagel
- cream cheese and cranberry sauce on a toasted English muffin
- Swiss, cheddar or Jack cheese cubes, whole wheat crackers and an orange
- toasted peanut butter and sliced banana sandwich
- a carton of yogurt and a small box of raisins
- egg, tuna or chicken salad in half a pita bread
- tuna salad with lettuce in a taco shell
- scrambled eggs with chopped tomatoes in half a pita bread
- pepperoni, dried fruit and a roll
- celery sticks filled with peanut butter or cheese spread or cream cheese, and a roll, cracker or muffin
- Boston Brown Bread spread with cream cheese mixed with honey

Good Morning Beverages

What refreshes more than a tasty morning drink? Juice is always a start-the-day favorite and juice combinations are unlimited, once you start thinking of all the possibilities. You might also like to try some interesting breakfast shakes for a frothy morning start. Some are breakfasts in a glass and make great eat-on-the-run meals even on the busiest morning. And of course hot morning beverages are always a favorite, especially hot chocolate. Create your own flavorful mixes ahead and just add boiling water to make a mug full of warm chocolate flavor.

Beverage Tips

- For variety at the breakfast table, use champagne, wine and parfait glasses to serve juices.

- Spark up any morning drink with a pretty, simple garnish:

  sprig of mint
  whole strawberry, slit to hang on edge of glass
  skewered pineapple chunks
  fruit kabobs
  lemon, lime or orange slices slit to hang on the edge of the glass, peels notched for a decorative touch

- A blender helps you create a tray full of frothy drinks in minutes.

- Freeze fruit juices in ice cube trays. Use to chill morning juice. Especially delightful in the summer.

- Make your own juice blends:

  pineapple-grapefruit   apple-orange
  cranberry-orange   orange-apricot
  pineapple-orange

Melon Cooler

The fresh taste of melon and lemon are a special blend.

1 cup cantaloupe, cut in small pieces
1 cup (8 ozs.) lemon flavored yogurt
½ tsp. sugar (optional)

Mix cantaloupe and yogurt in a blender.

Apricot Cooler

This is a cool, refreshing, sparkling morning drink.

1 (46 ozs.) can apricot nectar
1 (6 ozs.) can frozen orange juice concentrate
1 (28 ozs.) bottle 7-Up or ginger ale

In a large pitcher or punch bowl, mix apricot nectar and orange juice concentrate. This can be done early in the day and refrigerated. Just before serving, add 7-Up or ginger ale. To garnish, slice oranges and float on top, if using a punch bowl, or slit and hang on the side of each glass for individual servings. A sprig of mint at the side of the glass is a nice touch.

Tangy Citrus Cooler

Servings: 2

Creamy and delicious.

1 cup buttermilk
1 cup orange juice or tangerine juice
½ tsp. sugar
½ tsp. vanilla extract

In a blender mix buttermilk, juice, sugar and vanilla. Whirl until blended.

Variations:
- Use pineapple juice or a juice blend in place of orange juice.
- Use 2 cups buttermilk and ½ of a can (6 ozs.) lemonade concentrate or other concentrate. Omit sugar.
- Add an egg to any combination.

Breakfast Shakes

Try a breakfast blender shake. Simply combine ingredients in a blender, blend and enjoy!

Breakfast Nog   Servings: 1
1 egg
1 cup apricot nectar, apple juice or
    cranberry juice
½ cup nonfat dry milk powder
½ tbs. sugar
½ tsp. vanilla

a la Natural Nog   Servings: 1
1 egg
1 cup milk
1 tbs. honey, molasses or sugar
1 tsp. vanilla
nutmeg, cinnamon, apple pie spices

Orange Juliette   Servings: 2
1 (6 ozs.) can frozen orange juice
    concentrate
1 cup plain lowfat yogurt
½ cup milk
1 tbs. wheat germ

Sunrise Fruit Freeze   Servings: 2
1 cup plain or flavored yogurt
1 cup fresh or frozen fruit:
    strawberries, blueberries, peaches
1 tbs. sugar (optional)

Eggnog

Servings: 1

1 egg
1 cup milk
1 tbs. honey
1 tsp. vanilla

Fruit Flip

Servings: 1

½ cup fresh or frozen fruit:
    strawberries, raspberries, peaches
1 cup milk **or** yogurt
1 tbs. honey

Cranberry Spritz

Servings: 12

Sweet cran-raspberry juice, tart grapefruit juice and the bubbles of soda make this a hit.

2 cups cran-raspberry juice
4 cups grapefruit juice
2 cups club soda or sparkling water

Mix cran-raspberry juice and grapefruit juice together in a large pitcher. Just before serving, pour in club soda or sparkling water.

Tip: Add a little spark to almost any juice by mixing with equal parts chilled ginger ale or sparkling water. Or add 1 bottle of champagne or sparkling wine to each quart of juice.

Zippy Tomato Juice

This tangy vegetable starter makes an unusual morning beverage.

5-6 slices (¼" each) peeled cucumber
1 tsp. dill weed
1 tbs. lemon juice

2 ice cubes
1½ cups chilled tomato juice

In a blender, combine cucumber, dill, lemon juice and ice cubes. Blend 1 minute. Add tomato juice and blend a few seconds. Serve with a slice of unpeeled cucumber, cut and hung on the rim of the glass.

Pineapple Smoothie

A thick, tropical favorite.

1 (13½ ozs.) can pineapple pieces, chilled
2 tbs. sugar
½ cup orange juice

In a blender, combine pineapple, sugar and orange juice. Blend until smooth and serve.

Mexican Hot Chocolate

A hint of spice enhances this foamy hot chocolate. Serve with cinnamon sticks for stirring.

4 ozs. unsweetened chocolate
¼ cup sugar
2 tbs. cinnamon
2 quarts milk
8 cinnamon sticks
whipped cream (optional)

Combine ingredients in the top of a double boiler. Cook over hot water until chocolate is melted. Beat with a wire whisk until hot and foamy.

Tip: Whipping the milk as it heats prevents "skin" from forming on top.

Hot Chocolate Mixes

With a delicious variety of mixes you can serve a different flavored chocolate every day! A jar of any of these mixes makes a welcome gift, too.

Mint Hot Chocolate Mix
2½ cups mix

1 (6 ozs.) pkg. mint chocolate chips
1½ cups instant nonfat dry milk powder

Chop chips and milk together in a blender or food processor until ground. Store mix in a tightly covered jar. To serve, place 3 heaping tablespoons in a cup or mug and add 6 ozs. boiling water, stirring well to mix.

Variations:
- **Marshmallow Hot Chocolate.** Add ½ cup miniature marshmallows.
- **Hot Milk Chocolate.** Use milk chocolate chips in place of mint chips.
- **Spiced Hot Chocolate.** Use semisweet chocolate chips and add ½ tsp. cinnamon.
- **Mocha Hot Chocolate Mix.** Use semisweet chocolate chips and add ¼ cup instant coffee powder.

Mocha Mix

Here's a delightful blend of chocolate, coffee and cinnamon.

½ cup unsweetened cocoa
1 cup sugar
¾ cup nonfat dry milk powder

¾ cup nondairy creamer powder
½ cup instant coffee powder
1 tsp. cinnamon

Combine all ingredients well in a food processor or blender. Store mix in airtight containers. To serve, place 3 heaping tablespoons of mix in a cup and add 6 ozs. boiling water.

Variations:
Add any of the following extracts to the sugar in this recipe. Mix well to distribute extract evenly. Allow mixture to dry (an hour or more) and then proceed with the recipe.
- **Mint Mocha Mix.** Add ½ tsp. mint extract.
- **Almond Mocha Mix.** Add ½ tsp. almond extract.
- **Orange Mocha Mix.** Add ½ tsp. orange extract.

Mulled Pineapple Juice

A spicy change from usual morning drinks.

1 (46 ozs.) can pineapple juice
3 cinnamon sticks
8-10 cloves
5 whole allspice

Pour pineapple juice into a 2-quart saucepan. Add cinnamon sticks, cloves and allspice. Simmer 5 minutes. Remove spices and serve warm.

Tip: Place cinnamon sticks, cloves and allspice in a tea-bell or tie in cheese-cloth to simmer with juice.

Quick Cinnamon Cider

A sweet and spicy drink to serve on cool fall mornings.

1 quart apple cider
⅓ cup cinnamon red hot candies

Heat cider and cinnamon red hots until candy is melted and cider is hot. Pour into warm mugs.
Tip: For one serving, add 1 cup juice to 2 tsp. cinnamon red hots.

Hot Apple Toddy

Old fashioned flavors with the scent of apple pie.

4 cups apple cider
2 tbs. maple syrup
1 tsp. apple pie spice

4 slices orange or lemon
4 cinnamon sticks

Heat apple cider just to boiling. Add maple syrup and spices. Pour into warmed mugs and garnish with lemon or orange slice and cinnamon stick.

Breads, Muffins and Popovers

Breakfast just isn't breakfast to many morning diners without some form of bread. Here are plenty of ideas for everything from biscuits and fruit breads to puff pastry, muffins and popovers. Try the Currant Scones warm from the oven, or for a weekend treat serve Quick Cinnamon Rolls and be ready for rave reviews! Hot steamy muffins with butter are a delicious day's beginning. Or master the popover, easier to do than you think, and so impressive looking!

Basic Buttermilk Biscuits

10-12 biscuits

Biscuits and honey are a great morning team. My 13-year-old son Jason is the biscuit master at our house and quickly and easily creates these light-as-a-feather beauties that sing out "homemade."

2 cups all-purpose flour
3 tsp. baking powder
1 tsp. salt
½ tsp. baking soda
4 tbs. shortening
1 tbs. sugar
⅔ - ¾ cup buttermilk

In a small bowl, sift flour, baking powder, salt, soda and sugar. Using a pastry blender or two knives, cut shortening into flour mixture until it is the consistency of coarse cornmeal. Make a well in the center and pour in buttermilk. Mix lightly with a fork until dough leaves the sides of the bowl and begins to form a ball. Turn dough onto a lightly floured board. Gently knead 10-12 times. Roll or pat dough to 1" thickness. Cut with floured cutter. Bake in a 450° oven on a greased cookie sheet for 12-15 minutes or until tops are golden.

Variations:
- For cheese biscuits, add ¼ cup grated cheese (cheddar, Jack).
- For herb biscuits, add ½ tsp. thyme or marjoram to flour.

Biscuit tips:
- For biscuits that are light as air, use a light touch when mixing and kneading dough.
- For soft-sided biscuits, place biscuits close together on cookie sheet. For toasty sides, place biscuits 1" apart.
- Use a cookie cutter to make special shaped biscuits for special occasions.

Apple Bread

This good, solid bread is moist and sweet.

½ cup margarine
⅔ cup sugar
2 eggs, slightly beaten
1 tsp. vanilla
2 cups flour
1 tsp. baking powder

1 tsp. baking soda
½ tsp. salt
1 tsp. cinnamon
2 cups green apple, pared and coarsely grated
½ cup chopped walnuts
1 tbs. grated orange peel **or** lemon peel

In a medium bowl, beat margarine, sugar and eggs together until light. Sift dry ingredients together and alternately add with the apple, nuts and orange rind to cream mixture. Batter will be quite stiff. Turn into a well greased 9" x 5" x 3" loaf pan. Bake at 350° for 40 minutes or until done.

Melon with cottage cheese (page 2) ▶

Cinnamon Pull-Apart

Warm from the oven, this is a perfect Sunday morning treat.

2 loaves frozen bread dough
½ cup melted butter or margarine
½ cup sugar
2 tsp. cinnamon

¼ tsp. nutmeg
½ cup chopped nuts (walnuts, pecans, almonds or filberts)

Thaw dough according to package directions. Cut each loaf into 12 pieces and dip each piece first into melted butter, then into a mixture of sugar, cinnamon and nutmeg, and finally into nuts. Pile pieces into a greased bundt or angel food cake pan. Cover with a clean towel and allow to rise until double in size, about an hour. Bake at 350° for 30-35 minutes or until bread is golden and sounds hollow when tapped. Remove from pan immediately and place on a wire rack. Serve warm.

Variation:
- For a savory bread, use ½ cup Parmesan cheese in place of sugar, spices and nuts.

Best-Ever Banana Bread

Moist and filled with nuts, this is a good bread anytime.

2 ripe bananas, mashed
1½ cups sugar
½ cup vegetable oil
2 eggs
1 tsp. vanilla
¼ cup **plus** 1 tbs. buttermilk
1 tsp. soda
½ tsp. salt
1¾ cups flour
1 cup walnuts, chopped

In a medium bowl, mix bananas, sugar, oil, eggs and vanilla. Stir in buttermilk. In a small bowl, stir soda, salt and flour together. Add to banana mixture. Stir in nuts. Pour into a greased 9" x 5" x 3" loaf pan. Bake in a 325° oven for 1 hour and 20 minutes. *Do not double recipe.*

Orange Cranberry Bread

This bread is better the second day, and freezes well.

2 cups sifted all purpose flour
1 cup sugar
1½ tsp. baking powder
1 tsp. salt
½ tsp. soda
¼ cup margarine

1 tsp. grated orange peel
 cup orange juice
1 egg, beaten
1 cup fresh cranberries,
    whole or coarsely chopped
½ cup chopped walnuts

Into a medium bowl, sift flour, sugar, baking powder, salt and baking soda. Cut in margarine. In another small bowl, combine peel, juice and egg. Add to dry ingredients, mixing just until moistened. Fold in berries and nuts. Turn into a greased 9" x 5" x 3" pan. Bake at 350° for 50 minutes. Remove from pan to cool. Wrap and store overnight for best flavor. Makes one loaf.

Tips:
- Cranberries chop easily when frozen.
- Freeze bags of cranberries during the season and use them all year.

Currant Scones

Perfect with tea or coffee anytime, this old favorite is great with breakfast. They are best served warm.

2 cups all purpose flour
1 tbs. sugar
½ tsp. salt
1 tbs. baking powder
1 tsp. cinnamon
¼ cup margarine or shortening, cold

1 egg
½ - ⅔ cup milk
½ cup currants, dark raisins or
    golden raisins
melted butter
1 tbs. sugar

Into a large bowl, sift flour, sugar, salt and baking powder. Cut in cold margarine until mixture is crumbly. Add currants or raisins. In a small bowl, beat egg and milk. Add to flour mixture, stirring with a fork until soft dough forms. Do not overmix. Mixture will be soft. If too sticky, add 1 tbs. flour. Gently knead 4-5 times on a lightly floured board. Form into two balls and flatten on lightly greased cookie sheets. Brush tops with melted margarine and sprinkle with sugar. With a sharp knife, score the top of each round into 6-8 wedges. Bake in a 400° oven for about 15 minutes. Cut on scored lines.

Variations:
- **Ginger Spice Scones.** Add ½ tsp. ground ginger in place of cinnamon.
- **Orange Scones.** Add 2 tsp. grated orange rind to batter.

Tip: If not serving scones right away, wrap well and freeze. Warm in microwave oven. Or wrap in foil and heat at 350° for 5 minutes or until warm.

Irish Tea Bread

2 loaves

This flavorful authentically Irish cake-like bread is heavy with fruit. Wonderful spread with Orange Butter (page 162) and served with coffee or tea.

2 lbs. raisins
1 lb. dark brown sugar
2½ cups cold tea
4 cups **self-rising** flour
2 eggs, beaten
½ tsp. nutmeg
½ tsp. cinnamon

In a large mixing bowl, combine raisins, sugar and tea and allow to sit for 8 hours or overnight. Stir in 2 eggs, spices and flour. Mixture will be very moist. Bake in two greased loaf pans at 325° for 1½ hours or until done.

Tip: This bread freezes well.

Sausage Bread

A flavorful bread that is delicious served with scrambled eggs. Frozen bread dough makes it fast and simple to prepare.

1 loaf frozen bread dough, thawed
½ lb. bulk sausage
1 medium onion, chopped

Sauté sausage and onion. Drain off fat. Gently pat bread out to form a rectangle. Spread sausage to within 1 inch of edges. Roll dough in jelly roll fashion. Pinch gently to seal ends. Place seam side down in a 9" x 5" greased loaf pan. Bake at 350° for 35 to 40 minutes. Remove from pan and cool on wire rack before cutting.

Kringla

This puffy, flaky creation has been around for years and never fails to delight family and friends. The fun part is that it looks as if you've spent hours and it really is quick and easy.

Crust:
1 cup flour
2-4 tsp. water
½ cup butter

Puff:
1 cup water
½ cup butter
1 cup flour
3 eggs
½ - 1 tsp. almond extract

In a small bowl, mix butter and water to form a dough. Press onto cookie sheet in two 15" x 3" strips. In a medium saucepan, heat 1 cup water with ½ cup butter to boiling. Remove from heat and add 1 cup flour. Beat until smooth. Add eggs one at a time, beating hard after each addition. Add almond extract. Spread mixture on crust, making sure to cover all the edges. Bake at 375° for 45 minutes. Frost while warm. Cut each strip into 3" pieces.

Frosting:
1 cup powdered sugar
½ tsp. almond extract
1 tbs. butter
½ tbs. milk
½ cup slivered almonds

Mix powdered sugar, almond extract and butter, mixing well. Add milk one teaspoon at a time until glaze is of spreading consistency. Sprinkle with almonds.

Quick Cinnamon Rolls

This recipe is based on Davidson's famous cinnamon rolls. Adding honey to the butter adds a special flavor. Miranda, their wonderful baker, gave me a private lesson in cinnamon roll making early one morning and I learned how carefully and lovingly those rolls were created each day. A hot roll mix speeds up the process and the results are delicious! The frosting is optional.

Rolls:
1 pkg. hot roll mix
2 tbs. sugar
1 cup hot water
2 tbs. margarine or butter
1 egg

Cinnamon Mixture:
3 tbs. butter or margarine, softened
½ tsp. honey
⅓ cup sugar
1½ tsp. cinnamon
½ cup raisins

Frosting:
1 cup powdered sugar
1 tbs. butter or margarine, softened
2-3 tbs. milk or cream
½ tsp. vanilla

Lightly grease a 9" x 13" pan. In a medium bowl, pour roll mix, mixing in the provided yeast. Add sugar, stirring to mix. Stir in water, butter or margarine and egg. Stir until dough leaves side of bowl. Turn dough out onto a lightly floured surface. Form into a ball and knead for 5 minutes until dough is smooth. Rinse a bowl in hot water, dry, and turn upside down over dough. Allow to rest 5 minutes. Then, on a lightly floured surface, roll dough into a 15" x 10" rectangle. Mix butter or margarine with softened honey and spread on dough. In a small bowl, mix cinnamon and sugar. Sprinkle mixture evenly over buttered dough. Sprinkle with raisins. Beginning at shorter end, roll dough tightly. Pinch edges together to seal. Cut roll into 9 pieces. Place in prepared pan. Cover with clean towel. Let rise 30 minutes. Remove towel and bake at 350° for 20 to 30 minutes or until golden brown. Cool 1 minute. Remove from pan. Cool 10 minutes.

In a small bowl, mix powdered sugar, butter, milk or cream and vanilla until smooth. Spread over warm rolls to glaze.

Variations:
- Use frozen bread dough thawed, in place of hot roll mix.

Quick Cinnamon Rolls (continued)

- **Christmas Tree Bread.** Following the Quick Cinnamon Rolls directions, cut into 11 pieces. Arrange as shown in the illustration.
- **Golden Turkey Bread.** Double recipe. Cut two small dough strips. Roll one into a rope, twisting to form wattle for under beak. Pat second strip into triangle forming feet. Divide remaining dough in half. Form into rolls as in cinnamon roll recipe, cutting one into 6 pieces for feathers. Working directly on cookie sheet, coil the other roll to form head and body. Add wattle, feathers and feet and almond for eye, as shown. Allow to rise. Bake 30-35 minutes at 350°. Frost as desired.

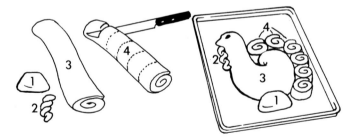

Strawberry Dumplings

My friend Pat Pfenning shared this old family recipe with me just for this book.

Dough:
3 eggs
1 tbs. sugar
2½ cups flour
water

sliced strawberries
sugar
cream or milk
buttered breadcrumbs

On a lightly floured surface, roll out dough to ¼" thickness. Cut into 5" squares. Place 1 heaping tablespoon of berries on dough. Sprinkle with 1 tsp. sugar. Bring four corners of dough together and pinch firmly, sealing well. Place in a pan of boiling water containing ¼ tsp. salt and 2 tsp. sugar. Cook 10 minutes. Serve in individual bowls, cover with warm cream or milk, and sprinkle with buttered bread crumbs.

Muffin Tips

- Do ahead! Stir dry ingredients together in a medium bowl in the evening. The next morning just combine with the liquid ingredients and bake.

For Perfect Muffins Every Time

- Stir all dry ingredients together in one bowl. In another bowl, mix liquid ingredients. Then make a well in the dry ingredients, add the liquid ingredients and stir just to moisten.

- Treat muffin batter gently. Don't overmix. Stir just 10-15 strokes, leaving the batter lumpy. Overmixing makes muffins tough.

- Lightly grease muffin pans or cups, or use a vegetable spray or paper liners.

- Fill muffin pans only ⅔ full.

- Always bake in a preheated oven.

- Allow muffins to rest in pans on a wire rack before removing so they don't break apart when taken out of pans. But do remove muffins from pans within 5 to 10 minutes to avoid soggy bottoms.

- Cool muffins completely before storing in airtight containers.

- Most muffins freeze well. Wrap cool muffins in plastic wrap and freeze for as long as 1 month.

- To reheat muffins, wrap muffins loosely in aluminum foil and heat in a 200° oven for 5 to 19 minutes. Reheat frozen muffins at 325° for 15 to 20 minutes. Or heat in a microwave.

- All muffin recipes here are for 3½- to 4-ounce muffin cups.

- **Streusel Topping**

  ½ cup chopped nuts
  ½ cup brown sugar
  3 tbs. flour
  1 tsp. cinnamon
  2 tbs. butter or margarine

  In a small bowl, mix together and sprinkle on top of muffin batter before baking. Tops 12 muffins.

Refrigerator Bran Muffins

Hot steaming muffins with melting butter are a good reason to get up! You can have them any morning with this ever-ready muffin batter in your refrigerator.

3 cups whole bran cereal
1 cup boiling water
2 eggs, slightly beaten
2 cups buttermilk
¾ cup salad oil
2 tbs. molasses (optional)

1 cup raisins, soaked and drained, **or**
    chopped apple, dates or nuts
2½ tsp. soda
½ tsp. salt
½ cup sugar
2½ cups all purpose flour, unsifted

In a large bowl, pour boiling water over cereal, stirring just to moisten evenly. Set aside until cool. In a medium bowl, beat eggs, buttermilk, oil and molasses if desired. In another bowl, stir soda, salt, sugar and flour together. Stir egg mixture into bran mixture. Add flour mixture, stirring just to combine. Bake muffins now or refrigerate the batter tightly covered for as long as two weeks. Stir batter to distribute fruit before using. Bake in paper-lined or greased and floured muffin tins at 375° for 20-25 minutes.

Banana split (page 4) ▶

Sausage Corn Muffins

12 muffins

Here's a breakfast muffin chock full of sausage with a lighter texture than most cornbread. This sweet cornbread is perfect served warm with Honey Nut Butter (page 162).

10 brown-and-serve sausages
1 (8½) ozs.) pkg. corn muffin mix
½ cup sour cream or sour half and half
2 eggs, slightly beaten
2 tbs. maple flavored syrup

Cook sausages according to directions, drain on paper towels, and cut into small pieces. Combine corn muffin mix, sour cream, eggs and maple syrup, stirring just until moistened. Carefully stir in sausages. Do not overmix. Allow batter to rest in bowl for 3 to 4 minutes before spooning into 12 greased or paper-lined muffin cups. Bake at 400° for 15 minutes.

Tip: Refrigerate any leftover muffins because of the meat they contain.

◀ **Sunrise Fruit Freeze (page 16) left, Tangy Citrus Cooler (page 15) center, Breakfast Nog (page 16) right**

Granola Muffins

Batter will keep two weeks in the refrigerator, so muffins can be ready in minutes.

4¾ cups flour
¼ cup wheat germ
2 tsp. cloves
2 tsp. cinnamon
½ tsp. nutmeg
1 cup white sugar

1 cup brown sugar
5 tsp. soda
4 eggs
1 cup oil
1 quart buttermilk
5 cups granola

In a large mixing bowl, stir together flour, wheat germ, cloves, cinnamon, sugar and soda. In another bowl, beat eggs; add oil and buttermilk and combine. Make a well in the center of flour mixture. Pour egg mixture into center and stir just until slightly combined. Be careful not to overmix. Fold in granola with a few quick strokes. Fill lightly greased or paper-lined muffin tins ⅔ full. Bake at 400° for 15 to 20 minutes.

Variations:

- Add 1½ cups grated apple with granola.
- Add ½ to 1 cup chopped dried apricots that have been soaked in ¼ cup hot water for at least 1 hour.
- Add 1½ cups cranberries coarsely chopped and mixed with ¼ cup sugar.
- Fill muffin cups half full of batter. Spoon 1 tsp. jam onto batter and cover with more batter until ⅔ full.
- Add 1½ cups raisins that have been covered with boiling water and then soaked for at least 1 hour, and ½-1 cup chopped walnuts, pecans or filberts.
- Add 2 tsp. grated orange peel to flour. Stir 1 tsp. orange marmalade into batter in each muffin cup. Add Streusel Topping (page 45) before baking.

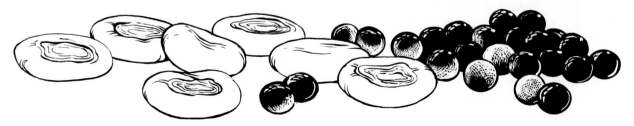

Blanche's Best Bran Fruit Muffins

36 muffins

My mother-in-law, Blanche Bauer, makes these wonderfully moist fruit-filled gems and always seems to have some ready in her freezer to serve to guests or to take to a friend as a treat. Although there are several steps, the recipe goes together easily.

2 cups All Bran
1 cup Bran Buds
1 cup boiling water
1 cup nuts
2 cups dried fruit,
    a mixture of prunes, raisins and dates
1 cup water
2½ cups flour

2½ tsp. soda
½ tsp. salt
½ cup (1 stick) margarine
1 cup brown sugar
2-3 eggs
1 tsp. vanilla
2 cups buttermilk

In a mixing bowl, combine All Bran and Bran Buds and pour boiling water over all. Set aside to cool. Add nuts to cooled mixture. In a small saucepan, place dried fruit and cover with water. Simmer for 10 minutes. Set aside to cool. In a mixing bowl, stir together flour, soda and salt. In another bowl, cream margarine, brown sugar, eggs and vanilla. Add buttermilk and combine. Make a well in the flour mixture and add creamed mixture. Add all of fruit, undrained. Stir in bran mixture just until combined. Bake at 350° for 20 to 25 minutes. Mixture will keep, tightly covered, in the refrigerator for 3 weeks.

Albertina's Brown Sugar Muffins

18 muffins

I always feel good about having lunch at Albertina's. All of the profits from the restaurant as well as the shops located in the old Kerr family home (you've heard of Kerr Jars) are donated to the Albertina Kerr Centers, dedicated to helping troubled children and their families in Portland. Ann Armstrong and her entirely volunteer staff have graciously offered two of their famous muffin recipes to be included here.

1 cup brown sugar
½ cup butter
1 egg
1 cup milk
½ tsp. salt

½ tsp. soda
1 tsp. baking powder
2 cups flour
½ cup chopped nuts
½ tsp. vanilla

In a medium bowl, cream sugar and butter. Add egg and milk, stirring well to combine. In another bowl, stir salt, soda, baking powder and flour. Add to sugar mixture. Stir in nuts and vanilla. Fill slightly greased, sprayed or paper-lined muffin cups ⅔ full. Bake at 425° for 12-15 minutes.

Albertina's Cheese Bacon Muffins

2 cups flour
3 tsp. baking powder
½ tsp. salt
¼ cup shortening
1 egg, beaten
1 cup milk
1 cup sharp cheddar cheese, shredded
4 strips of bacon, cooked crisp and crumbled

In a medium bowl, stir flour, baking powder and salt together. Cut shortening into dry ingredients until mixture resembles coarse corn meal. Stir in cheese and bacon. In a small bowl combine milk and egg. Add all at once to dry mixture, stirring just until moistened. Fill lightly greased, sprayed or paper-lined muffin cups ⅔ full. Bake at 400° for 20 to 25 minutes.

Blueberry Cinnamon Muffins

These are cake-like muffins brimming with blueberries, topped with brown sugar.

½ cup (1 stick) butter or margarine
1 cup sugar
2 egg yolks
⅓ cup sour cream or plain yogurt
1½ cups sifted all purpose flour
1½ tsp. baking powder

½ tsp. cinnamon
½ tsp. nutmeg
2 cups fresh or frozen blueberries
2 egg whites, stiffly beaten
brown sugar

In a medium mixing bowl, cream butter and sugar well. Add egg yolks and sour cream. Mix again. Into a medium bowl, sift flour, baking soda, cinnamon and nutmeg. Set aside 2 tbs. of the dry ingredients to toss with blueberries. Stir dry ingredients into creamed mixture. Wash, drain, pat dry, and flour blueberries. Fold into batter. Beat egg white and gently fold egg into batter. Spoon into paper-lined or greased and floured muffin tins. Sprinkle brown sugar over each muffin. Bake at 375° for 20 to 25 minutes.

Corn Muffin Pie

Here's a quick meal in a dish. This can even be served with maple syrup.

1 (8½ ozs.) pkg. corn muffin mix
2 eggs
½ cup sour cream
1 can whole kernel corn
1 pkg. brown-and-serve sausages

In a small bowl, stir corn muffin mix, egg and milk together just to blend. Stir in corn. Allow batter to rest a few minutes before pouring into a greased 9" pie plate. Arrange sausages spoke-fashion on top. Bake at 350° for 25 minutes.

Jan's Popovers

Jan has made her famous popovers every Sunday for more than 30 years, so she's the "resident expert." She says the secret to popovers that really poof is to bake them in heated glass custard cups and not to peek during the first 40 minutes. Her recipe using half milk and half water makes them as light as air.

2 eggs
⅔ cup flour
½ tsp. salt
½ cup milk and ½ cup water **or** 1 cup milk

In a medium bowl, mix eggs, flour, salt, milk and water, whipping well with a wire whisk. Or use a food processor, blender or electric mixer. Allow the mixture to rest for 5 to 10 minutes at room temperature. Lightly grease 4 custard cups, 10 ozs. each, place them on a cookie sheet and heat in the oven. Pour batter into the hot custard cups and bake at 400° for 40 minutes . Don't peek! After 40 minutes, make a slit in the side of each one with a knife to allow steam to escape. Turn heat down to 375° and continue baking for 15 to 20 minutes. Serve immediately with butter and jam or honey.

Tips:

- This recipe fills 12 muffin cups, 2½" each, **or** 9 custard cups, 5 ozs. each.
- For 1½" mini muffin pans, spoon 1½ tbs. batter into each cup. Bake for 23 minutes. Cut a 1" slit in top or side of each popover and bake an additional 5 minutes to dry.
- Lightly oil baking containers or spray with vegetable spray or popovers will stick.
- Popovers are at their very best served piping hot right out of the oven.
- If using a food processor or blender, blend just until smooth. Do not overbeat or popovers will not rise.
- Allow batter to rest at room temperature for 5 to 30 minutes.
- Bake in custard cups, cast iron popover pans or metal muffin pans.
- Fill only ⅔ full.

Do-Ahead Tip: Batter can be mixed and refrigerated for as long as 2 days.

Variations:
- **Bacon Popovers.** Add cooked, crumbled bacon to bottom of each greased cup or pan. Add batter and bake. Wonderful filled with scrambled eggs.
- **Cheese Popovers.** Add ½ cup shredded cheddar or Swiss cheese to batter.
- **Lemon Spice Popovers.** Add 1 tsp. grated lemon peel, 1 tsp. cinnamon and 2 tsp. sugar to batter.
- **Orange Almond Popovers.** Add ¼ cup ground, blanched almonds and 1 tsp. orange rind to batter.
- **Parmesan Popovers.** Add 3 tbs. Parmesan cheese to batter.
- **Spice Popovers.** Add 1 tsp. cinnamon and 2 tsp. sugar to batter.

Popovers Make a Perfect Holder:
- Fill with creamy chicken, ham, turkey or crab.
- Fill with creamy scrambled eggs.
- Fill with spinach souffle.
- Fill with sweetened fruit and sour cream, yogurt or whipped cream.
- Fill with ¼ cup chutney mixed with 8 ozs. softened cream cheese.

Fat-Free Spice Popovers

My cousin Marie is on a totally fat-free diet due to health problems. So I developed this popover recipe just for her and for all those who must be on special diets.

egg substitute to equal 2 eggs
⅔ cup all purpose flour
½ cup water
½ cup nonfat milk

1 tsp. salt
1 tsp. cinnamon
½ tsp. nutmeg
2 tsp. sugar

In a medium bowl, beat egg substitute, flour, water, milk, salt, cinnamon, nutmeg and sugar until well blended. Allow batter to rest for 5 to 30 minutes. Meanwhile, place 4 custard cups on a cookie sheet and heat in a 375° oven. When cups are hot, pour in batter, filling each cup ⅔ full. Bake for 30 minutes. Make a slit in the side of each popover with a knife and return to a 350° oven for 5 to 10 minutes. Serve immediately.

Breakfast Cookies and Bars

Everyone loves cookies. Remember sitting with a big glass of milk and a handful of Grandma's warm cookies, straight from the oven? Isn't it nice to know cookies can be good for you even for breakfast? Cookies are so easy to eat. Just grab one or two with a glass of milk and there's a healthy start even on the run. Here are some delicious and nutritious cookies filled with healthy ingredients. Try Oatmeal Breakfast Cookies or Carrot Nut Cookies or the fruit-filled Apple Butter Bars. Get creative and don't be afraid to adapt any of the recipes to create your own varieties. Add or substitute different nuts, chopped dried fruit, bran, oatmeal, coconut, wheat germ or sunflower seeds.

Apple Butter Bars

A moist and delicious center of spiced apple butter makes this a great start-the-day cookie.

¾ cup margarine
¾ cup brown sugar
1 cup whole wheat flour
¼ cup wheat germ
1½ cups rolled oats

1 tsp. cinnamon
½ tsp. nutmeg
¼ tsp. salt
¾ cup apple butter
½ cup raisins

In a medium bowl, cream margarine and brown sugar. In a second bowl, stir together flour, wheat germ, rolled oats, cinnamon, nutmeg and salt. Add to creamed mixture and stir just to combine. In a greased 9" x 9" pan, spread ½ the batter. Cover with a layer of apple butter and sprinkle with raisins. Top with remaining batter. Bake in a 375° oven for 25 to 30 minutes. Cut into 12 bars.

Granola Bars

This moist cookie is best cut and wrapped individually for a quick breakfast.

1 cup butter or margarine
1 cup brown sugar, firmly packed
1 cup orange juice
4 cups quick cooking rolled oats
1 tsp. vanilla
½ cup raisins
1 cup chopped walnuts
1 cup flaked coconut

In a medium saucepan, melt butter or margarine and add brown sugar and orange juice. Stir constantly until sugar melts. Add vanilla and stir. Remove from heat and add rolled oats, nuts and coconut. Spread in a 9" x 13" pan. Bake at 350° for 15 to 20 minutes. Cool slightly and cut into bars.

Hot Chocolate Mixes (page 21) ▶

Fruit-Bit Bars

You'll find a surprise of pieces of dried fruit in this healthy bar cookie.

¾ cup margarine
¾ cup brown sugar
1 egg
1 tsp. vanilla
1 cup whole wheat flour

¼ cup wheat germ
1½ cups rolled oats
1 tsp. cinnamon
½ tsp. nutmeg
1½ cups dried fruit, chopped

In a medium bowl, beat margarine and brown sugar until blended. Add egg and beat until fluffy. Stir in vanilla. Stir in flour, wheat germ, rolled oats, cinnamon and nutmeg. Stir in fruit bits. Press mixture into a lightly greased 9" x 13" pan. Bake at 375° for 10 to 12 minutes.

Do-Ahead Tip: Wrap cookies individually in plastic and then place in plastic freezer bags and freeze. In the morning, warm cookies in a microwave oven for a ''just made'' taste.

Oatmeal Breakfast Cookies

These are so good the kids will hardly believe they are good for you!

½ cup margarine
½ cup brown sugar
¼ cup granulated sugar
2 tbs. orange juice
1 tsp. vanilla
1 egg, beaten
½ cup whole wheat flour

½ tsp. baking powder
½ tsp. soda
½ tsp. salt
1 cup shredded coconut
1 cup quick cooking oats
1 cup chopped dates

In a medium mixing bowl, cream margarine, sugars and vanilla. Add beaten egg. Stir flour, baking powder, soda and salt together. Add to creamed mixture. Stir in coconut and quick cooking oats. Drop by tablespoons onto a greased cookie sheet. Bake in a 350° oven for 16 minutes. Cool 5 minutes on cookie sheet.

Apple Molasses Breakfast Cookies

15 cookies

This is a moist cookie that will last several days in the cookie jar if you can keep them around that long!

½ cup margarine
½ cup granulated sugar
½ cup brown sugar
1 egg beaten
½ cup whole wheat flour
½ cup wheat germ

½ tsp. baking powder
½ tsp. soda
½ tsp. salt
1½ cups oatmeal
2 tbs. apple juice
1 small apple, peeled and chopped (½ cup)

In a medium bowl, cream margarine and sugars. Add egg and stir to combine. Stir together flour, wheat germ, baking powder, baking soda and salt. Add to creamed mixture. Stir in apple juice and chopped apple. Drop by tablespoons onto a lightly greased cookie sheet. Bake in a 350° oven for 13 minutes.

Coconut Raisin Breakfast Nuggets

12-14 cookies

A sweet and flavorful cookie, great any time of the day!

½ cup margarine
½ cup brown sugar
1 egg
1 tbs. milk
1 tbs. molasses
¾ cup whole wheat flour

½ cup wheat germ
½ tsp. baking soda
½ tsp. salt
¾ cup coconut
½ cup chopped walnuts
½ cup raisins

In a medium bowl, cream shortening, sugar and vanilla. Add egg, milk and molasses. Stir together flour, wheat germ, soda, baking powder and salt. Add to creamed mixture. Stir in coconut, walnuts and raisins. Drop by tablespoons onto a greased cookie sheet. Bake in a 350° oven for 13 minutes.

Carrot Nut Cookies

Nutritious and delicious, these cookies are incredibly light.

1 (7½ ozs.) jar junior baby food carrots
1 cup margarine
¼ cup granulated sugar
½ cup brown sugar
1 egg
1 tsp. vanilla
¾ cup all purpose flour

1 cup whole wheat flour
¼ cup wheat germ
2 tsp. baking powder
½ tsp. salt
2 tsp. cinnamon
1 cup chopped walnuts
1 cup raisins

In a medium bowl, cream shortening, sugars and egg together. Add carrots and vanilla. Stir together flours, wheat germ, baking powder, salt and cinnamon. Add to creamed mixture. Stir in nuts and raisins. Drop by tablespoons onto a lightly greased cookie sheet. Bake at 350° for 14 to 16 minutes.

Cereals and Puddings

Cereal is one of the most popular breakfast items today, and I've included a Great Granola recipe and some cold and hot cereal tips. Look in the Breakfast Can Be Fun section and the It Doesn't Have to Look Like Breakfast section for more cereal ideas.

A bowl of pudding is a wonderful "warm and fuzzy" breakfast dish. Rice, bread and noodle puddings are rich with milk, eggs and spices, and you will find them here. Try the wonderful Bread Pudding from Davidson's for a special treat.

Great Granola

Be sure to make plenty of this versatile mixture. It's great for breakfast, as a portable snack, and in cookies, muffins and breads.

6 cups quick cooking or regular rolled oats
1 cup wheat germ
1 cup shredded coconut
1 cup sunflower seeds
1 cup chopped walnuts
1 cup sesame seeds

1 cup sliced almonds, broken
1 cup nonfat dry milk powder
1 cup vegetable oil
1 cup honey
2 tsp. ground cinnamon
2 tsp. vanilla

In a large bowl or pan, mix oats, wheat germ, coconut, sesame seeds, nuts and dry milk. Pour oil, honey, cinnamon and vanilla into a small pan and heat, stirring until hot but not boiling. Pour over oat mixture and stir until evenly moistened. Spread mixture on two large rimmed baking pans. Bake uncovered in a 200° oven about 1 hour, stirring every 15 minutes. Allow to cool thoroughly and then store in airtight containers. Will keep several weeks or freeze for longer storage.

Cold Cereal

Tips:

- Try apple, orange, or cranberry juice in place of milk on dry cereal for a new taste treat.
- To wean children from presweetened cereal, begin by mixing it half and half with unsweetened cereal, cutting back on the ratio until the switch is complete.

Toppings:

- fresh, canned or frozen fruit
- raisins or other dried fruit
- yogurt
- ice milk
- yogurt and honey

Hot Cereal

Tips:

- Add raisins or dried fruit to boiling water before adding cereal.

- Substitute fruit juice for water. Try apple juice, orange juice, or cranberry juice for a flavor surprise.

- Use your crockpot for an effort-free morning. The night before, lightly grease your crockpot, and follow the package directions for cooking the cereal. Cover and cook on low until morning.

Toppings:

- butter or margarine
- brown sugar
- cinnamon and sugar
- fresh fruit
- jams and preserves
- milk, half and half, cream or yogurt
- chopped nuts
- raisins or dried fruit bits
- ice milk or frozen yogurt or ice cream
- spices: allspice, apple pie spices, cinnamon, nutmeg, or pumpkin pie spice

Special Rice Pudding

This rich, delicious pudding is a wonderful morning treat or a welcome dessert.

3 cups milk
½ cup rice
¼ cup sugar
¼ tsp. salt
1-2 tbs. butter or margarine (optional)
¼ cup raisins, soaked and drained

2 eggs, well beaten
1 tsp. vanilla
2 tbs. sugar
2 tsp. cinnamon
⅛ tsp. nutmeg

In a medium saucepan, combine milk, sugar and salt. Heat just until small bubbles form around edge of pan. Stir in rice. Cover and cook over low heat for 35 to 45 minutes or until most of milk is absorbed and rice is tender. Stir in well beaten eggs. Return to low heat, stirring constantly, until mixture thickens. Stir in vanilla and raisins. In a small bowl, combine sugar, cinnamon and nutmeg. Pour pudding into serving dishes and sprinkle with cinnamon sugar mixture. Serve warm or chilled.

Variations:

- **Apple Rice Pudding.** Substitute dried apple for raisins.
- **Apricot Rice Pudding.** Substitute dried apricots for raisins.
- **Brown Rice Pudding.** Substitute ¾ cup brown rice for white rice.
- Add ½ cup seedless red or green grapes, halved.
- Add ½ cup kiwi fruit, pared and cut into chunks.
- Add ¼ cup mandarin oranges, well drained.
- Add ½ cup mixed dried fruit.
- Substitute brown sugar for white sugar.

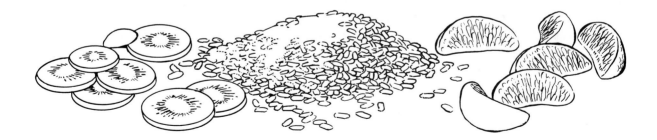

Quick Rice Pudding

This low fat recipe uses leftover rice. Cook up extra rice for dinner and then turn it into a creamy breakfast treat.

1 egg **plus** 1 egg white, **or** 2 eggs
3 cups cooked rice
2 tbs. sugar
2 cups nonfat milk
1 tsp. vanilla
¼ cup raisins

In a medium saucepan, beat egg and egg white slightly. Stir in rice, sugar, milk, vanilla and raisins. Place on heat and bring mixture just to boiling. Lower heat and cook, stirring constantly until mixture thickens (about 5 minutes).

Kugel Noodle Pudding

This is an old time favorite. If you haven't tried it yet, now is the time! Good for breakfast or dessert.

3 eggs
½ cup sugar
1 pint sour cream
1 pint cottage cheese

6 ozs. wide noodles, cooked
1 tbs. vanilla
¼ cup butter

In a 9" x 12" pan, melt butter in a 350° oven. In a large bowl, mix eggs, sugar, sour cream, cottage cheese, noodles and vanilla. Remove pan of butter from oven and pour in egg and noodle mixture. Bake at 350° for 45 minutes to 1 hour. Serve warm.

Variations:
- Add 1 tsp. cinnamon.
- Add ½ cup raisins.
- Add ½ cup chopped walnuts or almonds.

Bread Pudding From Davidson's

Servings: 12-16

Here in Portland everyone heads for Davidson's for their fabulous bread pudding. Owners Buzz, Gary and Gregg were kind enough to share their recipe with me, but note that the original depends on their day-old homemade cinnamon rolls (page 40). Of course that's part of the secret to this great recipe, but if you don't have rolls, use a rich day-old cinnamon raisin bread.

2½ cups day-old cinnamon rolls
   cut into ½" cubes, packed
⅓ cup raisins
8 large eggs
4½ cups milk

⅓ cup sugar
1 tbs. cinnamon
⅛ tsp. nutmeg
1 tsp. vanilla extract
half and half

Into a well greased 3-quart pan, pour cubed cinnamon rolls. Sprinkle raisins evenly over all. In a mixer, blend eggs, milk, sugar, cinnamon, nutmeg and vanilla, mixing well. Pour egg mixture over cinnamon rolls and raisins and allow to soak only 30 minutes. Bake in a 325° oven for 50 minutes. Remove from oven and let cool. Serve warm or cold with half-and-half. Reheat in a microwave on low until warm if desired.

Fruits

Fresh fruit simply cut or sliced makes a sweet and refreshing addition to any morning meal. Combinations of fruits can also add interest to breakfast. Here are some good-start-to-the-day recipes using fruit to add color and variety to your morning menus.

Fruit Tip: Make fresh fruit kabobs: choose any fresh fruit in season, such as melon, pineapple, and strawberries. Thread the fruits on wooden skewers, alternating colors.

Baked Applesauce Granola

Servings: 3-4

Served warm with a cream or yogurt topping, this delicious dish is a complete breakfast.

2 cups applesauce
½ tsp. cinnamon
⅛ tsp. nutmeg
2 tbs. brown sugar
⅓ cup raisins, soaked and drained
1 cup granola
1 tbs. wheat germ
yogurt or sour cream for topping

In a small oven-proof bowl, mix applesauce, cinnamon, nutmeg, brown sugar and raisins. Cover applesauce mixture with a layer of granola and sprinkle with wheat germ. Bake 20 minutes in a 350° oven. Top each serving with a dollop of yogurt or sour cream.

Granola Muffins (page 50) ▶

Strawberry Applesauce

Servings: 3-4

Strawberries add a colorful surprise to a bowl of applesauce.

½ cup sliced strawberries, fresh or frozen
1½ cups applesauce
sugar to taste

Combine strawberries and applesauce. Sweeten to taste.

Variation:
- Add ¼ tsp. cinnamon

Rosy Cinnamon Applesauce

Servings: 3-4

A warm and spicy breakfast fruit.

2 cups applesauce
2 tbs. cinnamon red hots

In a small pan, heat applesauce and cinnamon red hots until candy is melted. Serve warm, and add topping if desired.

Granola Baked Apple

The aroma of hot apple pie greets breakfast lovers with this flavorful morning treat.

4 large cooking apples
1 cup granola
1 tsp. cinnamon
¼ tsp. nutmeg
2 tbs. raisins or chopped dried fruit

water
½ cup sour cream or yogurt
brown sugar
nuts

Cut off the top 1" of each apple. Set aside. Using a spoon, scoop out pulp from apple, leaving ½" shell. Reserve pulp. Mix granola, cinnamon, nutmeg, raisins and chopped apple pulp. Fill apples with granola mixture. Place apples in a shallow baking pan and fill with 1" of water. Bake in a 400° oven for 25-30 minutes. Serve warm topped with sour cream or yogurt and sprinkled with brown sugar and nuts.

Variation:
• Add ½ tsp. peanut butter to granola before filling apples.

Tip: Cut scallops or points in top of the apple for a decorative touch.

Strawberry Supreme

A luscious treat during fresh strawberry season at breakfast, brunch or anytime!

1 quart fresh strawberries
1 pint sour cream or sour half and half
¾ cup brown sugar

Arrange bowls of strawberries, sour cream and brown sugar. Dip each strawberry first into sour cream and then into brown sugar.

Grapes Delight

Servings: 6-8

Ambrosia!

2 lbs. green grapes
1 cup (8 ozs.) sour cream

Stir grapes and sour cream together. Refrigerate covered overnight.

Coconut Banana Bites

An arrangement of orange wheels and Coconut Banana Bites makes an attractive and tasty breakfast or brunch fruit.

4 bananas, cut into 6 pieces each
1 cup sour cream

2 tbs. powdered sugar
1 cup flaked coconut

In a small bowl, mix sour cream or sour half-and-half and powdered sugar. Toast coconut in a 350° oven until lightly golden (about 5 minutes). Cool. Dip each piece of banana first into sour cream mixture, and then into coconut. Place in a single layer in a dish and refrigerate up to 24 hours.

Quick Fruit Compote

Sweet, spicy and special.

1 lb. mixed dried fruit
1½ cups (12 ozs.) lemon-lime soda
stick cinnamon

In a medium saucepan, place dried fruit, soda and cinnamon stick. Simmer 10 minutes. Chill. Serve chilled, garnished with mint leaves if desired.

Fruit Compote

A delightful do-ahead addition to brunch. This is an easy recipe to double or triple for large groups.

2 tbs. quick cooking tapioca
2 tbs. sugar
dash of salt
1½ cups water
1 (6 ozs.) can frozen orange juice
concentrate, partially thawed

1 (20 ozs.) can pineapple chunks
and juice
1 cup whole strawberries (fresh
or frozen)
1 large, firm but ripe banana

In a small saucepan, combine tapioca, sugar, salt and water. Stirring constantly, bring mixture to a full rolling boil. Remove from heat. Place orange juice concentrate in a medium bowl and add heated mixture, stirring to combine. Stir in pineapple and juice. Chill at least 4 hours, or overnight. Just before serving, add strawberries and bananas. Serve in stemmed glasses.

Variations:
- Add or substitute apricots, peaches and cherries.
- Add 1 tbs. apricot liqueur

Overnight Compote

Mix this easy combination and you'll have a healthy fruit course anytime. This compote can be refrigerated up to one week.

1 cup dried apricots
½ cup white raisins
1 cup dried apples
1 cup orange juice

Mix apricots, raisins, apple and orange juice. Refrigerate 8 hours or overnight.

Variations:
- Add other dried fruits, such as peaches or pears.
- Add a stick of cinnamon to mixture before refrigerating.
- Add 1 tbs. orange liqueur to mixture before refrigerating.

Curried Fruit

The exotic flavors of curry enhance humble canned fruit.

1 (29 ozs.) can peach halves
1 (20 ozs.) can pear halves
1 (16½ ozs.) can pineapple chunks
1 (16½ ozs.) can Bing cherries
⅓ cup butter
¾ cup brown sugar
1 tsp. curry powder

Drain all fruit well and dry on paper towels. Arrange in a 1½-quart casserole dish. Melt butter, add sugar and curry powder, and spoon over fruit. Bake at 350° for 1 hour. Refrigerate overnight. In the morning, bring fruit to room temperature and then bake for 30 minutes at 350°. Serve warm.

Cinnamon Spice Apple Rings

Pink apple rings are delicately spiced with cinnamon.

2 cooking apples
1 cup cranberry juice or water
⅓ cup sugar
1 tbs. cinnamon red hots

Cut apples into rings and core. Dip into cold salted water to prevent darkening. In a medium saucepan, bring cranberry juice or water and sugar to a boil. Add cinnamon red hots and stir until dissolved. Drop apple slices into syrup. Cover and simmer 5 minutes. Turn slices and continue cooking until tender. Serve hot or cold.

Variations:
• Or bake apples in syrup in a microwave for 2 minutes.
• Or bake apples in syrup in a covered dish in a 375° oven for 20 to 30 minutes.

Grapefruit

Half of a fresh grapefruit is a delicious and ever popular breakfast item. What a bonus that it is also so good for you! Of course grapefruit is a taste treat all by itself, but here are a few ideas to "gild the lily."

Toppings for Broiled Grapefruit (for each half grapefruit):

- 2 tsp. brown sugar
- 1 tbs. maple flavored syrup
- 1 tbs. apricot preserves
- 1 tbs. marmalade
- 2 tsp. liqueur, orange, almond or coffee flavored
- 2 tsp. sugar and a dash of cinnamon or nutmeg
- 1 tbs. each peanut butter and honey
- 1 tbs. each brown sugar and chopped nuts

Place under a preheated broiler, 4-5 inches from heat source. Broil for 3-4 minutes or until topping is bubbly.

Toppings for Chilled Grapefruit (for each half grapefruit):

- 1 tbs. orange flavored liqueur
- 1 tbs. apricot or peach flavored liqueur
- 1 tbs. cream de menthe

Lemon Yogurt Fruit Dip

Rich and creamy, this dip can be thinned with milk and used as a sauce.

1 (8 ozs.) pkg. cream cheese, softened
1 (8 ozs.) container lemon yogurt
1 tsp. grated lemon rind (optional)

drop lemon extract
1 tbs. honey

In a medium bowl, beat cream cheese until light and fluffy. Gently stir in yogurt a little at a time until well blended. Stir in lemon rind and honey. Refrigerate several hours or overnight. Serve as a dip for fresh apples, bananas, grapes, oranges, pears, plums, or strawberries.

Creamy Orange Sauce for Fruit

1 cup sour cream, sour half and half or yogurt
½ tbs. orange juice concentrate

In a small bowl, mix sour cream or sour half-and-half with orange juice concentrate. Serve as a dip for fruit.

Egg Dishes

Eggs are standard morning fare for many breakfast eaters, but there is no need to get in a rut! The variations for this protein-rich, economical food are many, and this section includes new ideas and old favorites. You'll find tips on buying, storing and preparing eggs as well.

For health-conscious people and those on special diets that restrict the consumption of egg yolks, egg substitutes can be used, or you may replace some whole eggs with egg whites. Either of these approaches works especially well with omelets, scrambled egg recipes, frittatas and stratas. A Skinny Strata is included as an example, and it's delicious!

Egg Tips

Buying Eggs

- When large eggs are $.90 a dozen, they are $.60 a pound.
  When large eggs are $.75 a dozen, they are $.50 a pound.

- Fresh eggs look rough and chalky. Older eggs look smooth and shiny.

- Place an egg in cool, salted water. If it SINKS to the bottom, it is fresh. If it RISES to the surface it is spoiled. Throw it away.

Storing Eggs

- Refrigerate eggs. One hour at room temperature is equal to a day in the refrigerator. Refrigerated eggs will keep for 4-5 weeks.

- Store eggs with the rounded end up.

- Don't wash eggs. This removes a protective coating.

- Eggs are porous, so don't store them near strong smelling foods.

- Store eggs in the carton rather than in egg cups on the refrigerator shelf.

- Yolks will keep for 2-3 days in the refrigerator if placed in a jar with a lid, covered with water.

- Whites will keep for 10 days in the refrigerator if stored in a covered jar.

- Both whites and yolks can be frozen.

Preparing Eggs

- Use a small funnel to separate whites and yolks.

- To keep eggs from cracking when placed in boiling water, pierce one end with a pin. And make sure eggs are room temperature before boiling.

- Use medium to large eggs for recipes. Extra large eggs may throw the recipe off and, for example, cause cakes to fall.

- For best results, use eggs at room temperature for baking.

- Use egg whites at room temperature for greatest volume when beating. Be sure to use totally clean bowls and beaters. No grease. No plastic. Don't beat the whites until they are dry. They should still be shiny.

- When boiling or poaching eggs, heat on simmer. High heat will toughen eggs.

- Never cook an egg in its shell in a microwave oven. It will explode. And always prick the egg yolk to allow steam to escape or it is likely to explode. A terrible mess!

Shirred Eggs

These baked eggs are an efficient way to prepare eggs in quantity.

For each serving:

2 eggs
salt
pepper

1 tbs. cream or milk
1 tsp. butter

Grease a ramekin or custard cup for each serving. Break eggs and slip them into each ramekin. Sprinkle with salt and pepper. Top each with 1 tbs. cream or milk. Dot with 1 tsp. butter. Bake at 350° until whites are set and yolks are soft and creamy, about 15 minutes. Serve immediately.

To bake in a microwave, prick the membrane that covers the yolk, and cover ramekin or custard cup loosely with plastic wrap. Cook for 2½ to 3 minutes. Remove from oven and allow to stand 1 minute.

Variations:
- Lightly sprinkle the bottom of each custard cup with herbs or Parmesan cheese.
- Add slices of precooked sausage links to the bottom of the custard cup or the top of the egg before cooking.

Cream Cheese Scrambled Eggs in Toast Cups

Servings: 4

Creamy eggs are served in tender little bread cups.

1 (3 ozs.) pkg. cream cheese, softened
¼ cup milk
4-6 eggs
1 tsp. chopped chives

1 tsp. salt
2 tbs. butter
4 slices of bread, crusts removed
   and buttered

Beat cream cheese until smooth. Gradually add milk. Add eggs, chives and salt. Beat with a fork or whisk until foamy. Melt butter in a frying pan. When sizzling, pour in egg mixture. Cook over medium heat, stirring and moving eggs from center and from sides until eggs are thick and creamy. Serve in toast cups and sprinkle with more chives.

Toast Cups:

Butter both sides of bread. Push bread into lightly greased muffin cups so that corners form points. Bake at 350° until golden brown. Toast cups can be made ahead and reheated just before serving.

Poached Eggs

Heat water 1½" deep in a frying pan to just simmer (bubbles forming on bottom of pan). Add 1 tbs. vinegar. Carefully break each egg into water. Simmer gently for 3 to 5 minutes, or until whites are firm. Remove with slotted spoon and drain on paper towels. Serve on toast.

Microwave Poached Eggs

In a small custard cup, bring ⅓ cup water to boil in microwave. Carefully break an egg into the water. Prick the yolk. Cover and cook 1 minute. Keep covered and allow to stand 1 minute.

Do Ahead Poached Eggs

Here's a great idea for entertaining. Eggs can be poached up to 24 hours before serving. Poach eggs as above. Remove from water and immediately plunge eggs into a bowl of cold water. Cover and refrigerate. When ready to serve, transfer eggs into a bowl of hot tap water for 10-15 minutes until eggs are hot.

Zucchini Frittata

This flavorful egg and vegetable dish is quick and easy. And you can freeze it after it is baked and cooled and reheat it at another time.

3 cups thinly sliced unpeeled zucchini
½ medium onion, chopped, **or**
   equivalent dried minced onion
1 cup biscuit mix
½ cup salad oil
½ cup Parmesan cheese

4 eggs, slightly beaten
pepper to taste
2 tsp. dried oregano
⅓ cup fresh **or** 2 tbs. dried parsley
garlic powder
dash of nutmeg

In a medium bowl, mix zucchini, onion, biscuit mix, salad oil and Parmesan cheese. Add eggs, pepper, oregano, parsley, garlic powder and nutmeg. Pour mixture into a lightly oiled 8" x 8" glass baking dish or a 9" pie plate. Bake at 350° for 25 minutes or until set and golden. Cool 10 minutes and cut into squares. Serve warm.

Omelets

Omelets are one of the most popular ways to serve eggs. They can be simple or elaborate, savory or sweet and are perfect for breakfast, lunch or dinner or for a snack anytime. Isn't it nice they are so easy to make!

For each serving:

2 eggs
2 tbs. water
¼ tsp. salt
dash pepper
1 tbs. butter

In a small bowl, beat eggs, water, salt and pepper with a fork. Heat a 7"-8" skillet over medium heat. Add butter and heat until sizzling. Pour in egg mixture. After about 5 seconds, with the side of a fork or with a pancake turner, carefully push cooked portions at edges to center to allow uncooked portions to flow to bottom, while shaking the pan and sliding it back and forth over the heat. This will keep the egg mixture moving so that it won't stick or overcook. While top is still moist and creamy-looking, add filling if desired. Fold in half or roll, turning onto plate quickly.

Tips:

- Prepare all filling ingredients before beginning to cook omelet.
- Cut up omelet ingredients into medium to small pieces.
- Omelets must be served immediately. Serve on warm plates.

For Fillings, Add:

- sautéed fresh or canned mushrooms
- sautéed onion
- tomatoes and sautéed green pepper
- cooked spinach
- cooked artichoke hearts
- cheeses — Parmesan, cheddar, Swiss, Jack, cream cheese, cottage cheese or ricotta
- herbs — tarragon, dill, oregano
- cooked, drained and crumbled bacon or sausage
- smoked salmon
- cooked shrimp
- salsa
- drained canned fruit or chopped or sliced fresh fruit
- jelly, jam or preserves

Sausage Strata

Servings: 4-6

This tasty do-ahead layered breakfast casserole can be easily changed. For example, substitute ham for sausage and Jack cheese for cheddar.

1 lb. bulk pork sausage, lightly cooked
½ lb. sharp cheddar cheese, shredded (2 cups)
6 slices firm day-old bread, cubed
4 eggs, beaten
4 cups milk
½ tsp. dry mustard

Drain sausage. In a 2-quart lightly greased casserole, alternate layers of sausage, cheese, and bread. Beat eggs, milk and mustard together. Pour over casserole. Refrigerate overnight. Bake at 375° for 1 hour.

Sausage Puff

This strata dish is also tasty with cooked bulk sausage in place of brown-and-serve.

6 English muffin halves
12 brown-and-serve sausages
4 eggs
2 cups milk
dash salt and pepper
½ lb. (2 cups shredded) cheddar cheese

In a small bowl, beat eggs with milk, salt and pepper. In the bottom of a 9" x 9" baking pan, arrange and cut muffins to fit. Arrange sausages on top of muffins. Pour milk and egg mixture over. Sprinkle with cheese. Refrigerate for 8 hours or overnight. Bake in a 325° oven for 45 minutes.

Brunch Puffs

A wonderful company dish with several variations.

12 puff pastry patty shells
6 ozs. bulk sausage, cooked
1 cup sour cream or sour half and half
6 ozs. shredded Swiss or Jack cheese
1 egg, beaten
2 tbs. flour
2 tbs. dry white wine
3 green onions, chopped (about ½ cup)
½ tsp. garlic powder
¼ tsp. dried basil
paprika
parsley

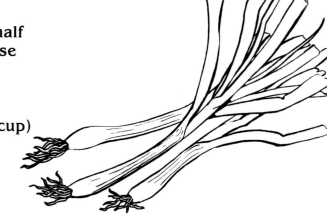

Bake patty shells according to package directions. Carefully remove pastry caps and set aside. Remove doughy centers and discard. Place shells on a baking sheet. Combine ham, sour cream, cheese, egg, wine, green onions, garlic powder and dried basil. Pack shells with filling. Sprinkle with paprika. Bake in a 325° oven for 30 to 40 minutes or until mixture is bubbling. Remove from oven and sprinkle with chopped parsley to garnish. Top with pastry cap if desired.

Variations:
- Use Italian sausage or hot sausage.
- Substitute ½ cup chopped ham for sausage.
- Substitute ½ lb. bacon cooked, drained and crumbled for sausage.
- Add ¼ cup grated Parmesan cheese.
- Add 1 tsp. prepared French mustard.

Do-Ahead Tip: Bake patty shells and prepare filling a day ahead. Fill shells and bake just before serving.

Deviled Egg Dish

This is another do-ahead dish, and it's simple enough for family and fancy enough for company.

8 hard cooked eggs
2 tbs. mayonnaise
2 tbs. cottage cheese
1 tsp. prepared mustard
salt and pepper
garnish: chopped parsley

Cut eggs in half and remove yolks. In a small bowl, mash well with mayonnaise, cottage cheese, mustard, salt and pepper. Refill whites with mixture. Put halves together. Place eggs in a lightly greased casserole dish. Pour sauce over and sprinkle with ½ cup grated cheese. Heat in a 350° oven for 15-20 minutes. Garnish with chopped parsley.

Sauce:

4 tbs. butter
4 tbs. flour
½ tsp. salt
2 cups milk or cream
1 tsp. dried minced onion
2 tbs. sherry
1½ cups shredded cheddar cheese

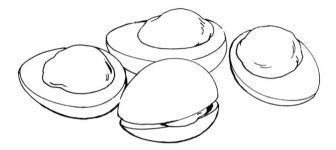

In a small frying pan, melt butter. Stir in flour and salt and cook until mixture bubbles. Remove from heat and add milk or cream, minced onion and sherry. Return to heat and cook until mixture thickens. Stir in 1 cup shredded cheese.

Variations:
- Add ½ cup sliced cooked or canned mushrooms to sauce.
- Add ½ tsp. curry powder to sauce.

Do-Ahead Tip: Prepare eggs and sauce a day ahead. Heat eggs with sauce in a 350° oven for 15 to 20 minutes or until hot.

Scrambled Eggs Fajitas

Arrange all the fillings in bowls and let everyone create a personalized Mexican breakfast. Fun for a party for all ages!

8 (7") tortillas
1 lb. bulk pork sausage **or**
  ground beef and chorizo
1 medium onion, chopped

butter or margarine
6 eggs
4 green onions, sliced
⅓ cup cheddar **or** Jack cheese
⅓ cup sour cream

1 (4 ozs.) can green chilies, cut up
1 (7 ozs.) can black olives, sliced
green onions, chopped
salsa
refried beans
Jack cheese, shredded
cheddar cheese, shredded
1 cup sour cream
chopped tomato

Wrap tortillas in foil and heat in a 300° oven for 10 to 15 minutes. Or wrap in plastic wrap and heat in a microwave oven. Cook sausage or ground beef with onion. Drain on paper towels. Place in a bowl and keep warm. Beat eggs, sour cream and green onions. Add butter to a frying pan and cook eggs, stirring.

Add cheeses. Arrange chilies, olives, green onions, salsa, refried beans, cheeses, sour cream and tomato in small bowls. To make each fajita, fill a warm tortilla with your choice of filling, eat with a knife and fork or fold into a pocket and eat.

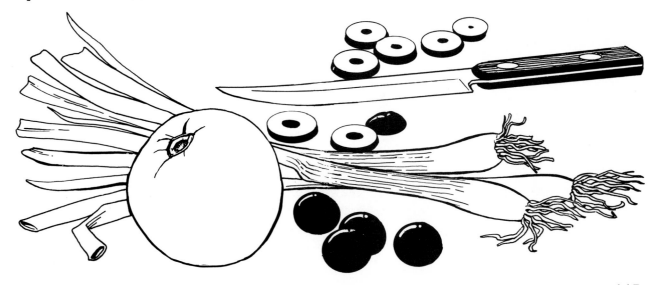

Egg Roll Quiche

Egg roll wrappers found in the produce department form the instant crust for this delicious time-saver.

12 egg roll wrappers
3 eggs, slightly beaten
1 cup milk
1 tbs. dried minced onion
salt and pepper
1 cup shredded cheddar cheese
6 slices bacon, cooked, drained and crumbled **or**
   ½ cup finely chopped ham
2 tbs. dried parsley flakes
paprika

Lightly grease muffin tins. Gently press an egg roll skin into each muffin cup. You may want to trim the skin to fit the cup. Set aside. Sprinkle cheese into each lined cup. Mix eggs, milk, minced onion and pepper. Pour egg mixture over cheese. Sprinkle each with bacon, minced parsley and paprika. Bake at 325° for 10-15 minutes.

Variation: For smaller quiches, use wonton skins and smaller muffin tins. Bake at 325° for 7-10 minutes. Can also be served as an appetizer.

Do-Ahead Tip: Baked quiche may be refrigerated for 24 hours or frozen. To freeze, place cooled quiches on a cookie sheet. Place in the freezer and freeze until firm. Place quiche in freezer containers and seal. To serve, heat frozen quiche uncovered at 325° for 10 minutes, or heat at low power in a microwave oven for 3 to 5 minutes.

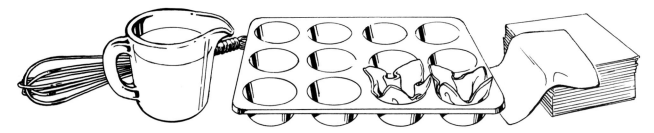

Eggs Benedict in Puff Pastry

Servings: 6

6 frozen pastry shells
6 eggs
6 slices Canadian bacon, heated

Bake pastry shells according to package directions, slightly undercooking so that shells are only light brown. Cool. Remove tops and carefully remove doughy middle, being sure not to make holes in sides of shell. If there should be a hole, patch with a piece of doughy middle. Place shells on a cookie sheet and crack an egg into each one. Gently pour 1 tbs. cream or half and half on top of each egg. Bake in a 300° oven for 30 minutes or until eggs are set. Meanwhile, heat Canadian bacon. To serve, place each pastry shell and egg on a piece of bacon; pour Hollandaise sauce over each serving.

Easy Blender Hollandaise Sauce:
3 egg yolks
1 tsp. dry mustard
1 tbs. lemon juice
1 cup (½ lb.) butter, melted and hot

In a blender or food processor, blend egg, dry mustard and lemon juice. While on highest speed, add melted butter, beginning with just a few drops at a time and increasing to a steady stream as mixture thickens. Serve immediately.

Tip: Prepare Hollandaise Sauce several hours ahead and keep warm in a vacuum bottle until serving time.

Variations:
- **Traditional Eggs Benedict.** Toast English muffins, place a piece of cooked Canadian bacon on each half, top with a poached egg and cover with Hollandaise Sauce.
- Prepare pastry shells, fill with scrambled eggs and cover with Hollandaise Sauce.
- **Hot Potato Benedict.** Scramble 4-6 eggs with 1 cup cubed ham. Open 4 baked potatoes, fluff insides gently, and spoon in egg mixture. Cover with Hollandaise Sauce.

Skinny Strata

Here's a low fat strata.

egg substitute to equal 4 eggs
4 slices French bread, cut into cubes
1 cup nonfat milk or low fat milk
1 can sliced mushrooms
1 tsp. dry mustard
1 cup smoked turkey breast, diced
1 cup low fat cheddar cheese, shredded
4 green onions, sliced **or** 2 tbs. dried minced onion

Beat egg substitute, milk and dry mustard together. In a well greased 2-quart casserole, layer half the bread cubes, half the mushrooms, turkey, onion and cheese. Repeat layers ending with cheese. Pour egg mixture over all. Refrigerate several hours or overnight. Bake in a 325° oven for 25 minutes.

Wonton Quiche (page 115) ▶

Fantastic Mexican Egg Dish

Servings: 6-8

The flavors of eggs, sausage and cheese are enhanced with a touch of spice from salsa. Garnish this pretty dish with chopped tomatoes and green onions.

6 eggs
3 tbs. sour cream
½ lb. bulk pork sausage
1 medium onion, chopped
¼ lb. sliced fresh mushrooms

¼ - ½ cup salsa
8 ozs. medium or sharp cheddar
   cheese, shredded
8 ozs. Monterey Jack cheese, shredded

Beat eggs and sour cream well. Pour into a greased 1½-quart pan and bake at 400° just until set, about 7 to 10 minutes. Don't overcook. Allow to cool slightly. Meanwhile, sauté sausage, chopped onion and mushrooms. Drain on paper towels. Spread sausage over cooked egg. Spread salsa over all. Layer cheddar and Jack cheese. This casserole may be refrigerated at this point. To serve, bake uncovered at 300° for 30 minutes. Remove from the oven and allow to sit for 10 minutes before cutting into squares to serve.

Garnish: Arrange rings of chopped green onion, chopped tomato and black olives. Top with sour cream. Arrange taco chips standing around the outside edge of casserole if desired.

Quick Quiche

This quiche goes together in minutes and makes its own crust while baking.

½ cup biscuit mix
3 eggs
½ cup butter or margarine, melted
1½ cups half-and-half or milk
¼ cup Parmesan cheese
1 tbs. dried minced onion
½ tsp. dried mustard
¼ tsp. salt
½ tsp. Italian seasonings (optional)
dash pepper
dash nutmeg
1½ cups shredded Swiss or Monterey Jack cheese
1 cup diced ham

In a medium bowl, mix biscuit mix, eggs, butter, half and half or milk, Parmesan cheese, onion, mustard, salt and pepper. Or mix in a blender or food processor for 30 seconds. Sprinkle cheese and ham on the bottom of a lightly greased 9" pie plate or fluted quiche dish. Pour egg mixture over all. Bake at 350° for 45 minutes.

Variations:
- Substitute 6 ozs. cooked bulk sausage for ham.
- Substitute 8-10 slices of bacon, cooked and crumbled, for ham.
- Substitute 1½ cups cheddar cheese for Swiss.
- Add 1 pkg. frozen spinach, thawed and squeezed dry.
- Add 1 medium onion, chopped, sautéed and drained.
- Add ½ cup sliced mushrooms, sautéed and drained.

Cheese Pie

This crustless quiche is a sure hit for family or company breakfasts.

4 eggs, slightly beaten
4 tbs. flour
1 cup milk
½ cup sour cream

¼ - ½ cup Parmesan cheese
1 cup Swiss cheese, grated
1-2 tsp. dried minced onion

In a medium bowl, mix eggs, flour, milk, Parmesan cheese, Swiss cheese and minced onion. Pour into lightly greased quiche dish or pie plate which holds 1½ quarts. Bake at 325° for 35 to 40 minutes or until puffed and golden.

Variations:
- Add ½ cup chopped ham.
- Add 4 slices bacon, cooked and crumbled.
- Add 1 pkg. frozen chopped spinach, thawed and squeezed dry.
- Add 1 can sliced mushrooms or ½ cup fresh sautéed mushrooms.
- Add ½ tsp. dried thyme.

Do-Ahead Tip: Prepare mixture and pour into greased pans. Cover with plastic wrap and refrigerate overnight. Allow to sit at room temperature before baking.

Potatoes and Meats

A breakfast book has to have a section on potatoes and meats! Somewhere in my heritage there must be some Irish, because I do love potatoes in just about any form. As I was working on this book, a friend reminded me not to forget to include potatoes, which is exactly what I had done. Everyone seems to love potatoes with breakfast. So here are potatoes, together with some fast-to-fix meat ideas.

Fried Potatoes

Delicious, nutritious potatoes give you energy all through the day. These are wonderful with eggs any style, but a meal alone.

4 red potatoes, cooked with skins and sliced ¼" thick
1 medium onion, sliced
1-2 tbs. vegetable oil
1 tbs. butter
½ cup shredded cheddar cheese

In a medium oven-proof frying pan, sauté onions in oil until limp and transparent. Add sliced cooked potatoes. Sauté in oil and butter, turning until golden brown. Sprinkle with cheese. Cover and cook over low heat just until cheese melts. Or if using an oven-proof frying pan, melt cheese under broiler.

Potato Pancakes

Simple and delicious, these side dish potatoes are especially good served with applesauce.

2½ cups raw potato, coarsely shredded
1 small onion, grated
1 tsp. salt
⅓ - ½ cup flour
dash pepper
1-2 eggs
2 tbs. salad oil
applesauce

Thirty minutes before serving, mix potatoes, onion, salt, flour, pepper and egg in a medium bowl. Preheat a skillet over medium-high heat until a drop of water bounces on the surface. Place 2 tbs. oil in the skillet. Make pancake shapes from potato mixture. Fry, turning once, until both sides are crisp and golden, about 5 minutes on each side. Drain thoroughly on paper towels. Place on a warm platter and serve with hot or cold applesauce.

Twice-Baked Potatoes with Egg and Cheese

Servings: 2

One morning on AM Northwest *I had the pleasure of meeting Sheila Lukins of the* Silver Palate Cookbook. *She is a delightfully warm and friendly woman and within minutes I felt we'd known each other a long time. I was working on this book and Sheila was encouraging and sincerely interested. As we chatted I mentioned that I wanted to include a breakfast potato section, and she was quick and generous with ideas for me. She suggested I work on a restuffed baked potato with an egg baked inside. Here it is. A potato lover's breakfast dream!*

2 large baking potatoes
4 tbs. sour cream
½ tsp. salt
¼ tsp. onion salt
herbs to taste

2 eggs
2 tbs. cream or milk
dash of salt and pepper
4 tsp. Parmesan cheese

Bake potatoes in an oven or microwave. While hot, cut open, being careful to leave bottom and sides of skin intact. Carefully scoop out contents of each potato and mash with 2 tbs. sour cream, salt, onion salt and herbs if desired. Spoon mixture back into potato shells and form a well in the center of each to hold egg. To bake, break an egg into the center of each potato, sprinkle with salt and pepper and cover with 1 tbs. cream or milk. Sprinkle with cheese. Bake in a 350° oven until eggs are set, about 15-20 minutes. Do not overcook. Eggs will continue to cook slightly once they are removed from the oven.

Variations:
- Sprinkle grated cheddar cheese over eggs the last few minutes of baking.
- Add 1 tsp. chopped chives for each potato.
- Sprinkle fresh or dried herbs on top of egg rather than adding to sour cream.

Do-Ahead Tip: Prepare potatoes with dinner potatoes the night before: mash as above, wrap and refrigerate. Add egg and bake in the morning.

Quick Oven Browns

Another great dish to serve with any style eggs.

½ cup chopped onion
1 tbs. butter or margarine
1 (10½ ozs.) can cream of celery soup
1 (3 ozs.) pkg. cream cheese
½ tsp. garlic powder
3-4 cups frozen hash browns
½ cup shredded cheddar cheese

Sauté onion in butter or margarine. Stir in undiluted soup and cream cheese cut into cubes. Cook stirring constantly until smooth and hot. Into a lightly greased 1 quart casserole, alternately layer potatoes, soup and cream cheese, ending with a layer of sauce. Bake in a 400° oven for 45 minutes. Sprinkle with cheese and return to oven until cheese melts.

Potato Egg Bake

Mashed potatoes, eggs and cheese combine for a satisfying morning meal.

2 cups mashed potatoes
2 tbs. sour cream or sour half-and-half
½ tsp. onion powder
⅛ tsp. nutmeg
4 eggs

½ tsp. salt
⅛ tsp. pepper
2 tbs. cheese
 (cheddar, Jack or a mixture)
1 tsp. paprika

In a medium bowl, mix potatoes, sour cream, onion powder and nutmeg. Grease 4 custard cups and place ½ cup mashed potato mixture in the bottom of each. Make a well in the center, break an egg into each well and sprinkle with salt, pepper, cheese and paprika. Place custard cups on a cookie sheet for ease in handling and bake in a 400° oven for 10 minutes or until eggs are set as desired.

Variations:
- Use instant mashed potatoes prepared according to package directions.
- For richer tasting potatoes, add 2 tbs. cream cheese to hot mashed potatoes.

Oven Broiled Bacon

This cooking method is easy because it requires no draining.

Place bacon on a preheated broiler rack or for small quantities, on a wire rack over a shallow pan. Broil 3½" - 4" from heat source for 2 to 3 minutes on each side, turning once.

Oven Baked Bacon

Baked bacon is easy and especially handy when preparing a large amount. Place unseparated bacon slices on a broiler rack or for a smaller amount on wire racks over shallow pans. Bake at 400° for 5 minutes. Separate bacon into strips. Bake for 15 minutes more. No turning is necessary. Drain on several layers of paper toweling and serve.

Bacon Curls

Make a pretty garnish by cutting a piece of bacon in half and rolling it into a loose curl. Push a toothpick through the curl and broil until done. Serves as part of a breakfast meat tray or as an edible decoration.

Bacon Tip: Cooked or uncooked bacon can be frozen, well wrapped, for a month.

Curly Ham

Lightly fry paper-thin slices of ham. The edges will curl for a decorative look.

Do-Ahead Sausages

A little effort ahead of time makes the job simple.

In a large skillet, place links with ¼ cup water. Cover and steam about 5 minutes. Drain and refrigerate up to 2 days. When ready to cook and serve, place sausages on a rack over a pan and bake at 350° for 10 minutes or until done.

Sausage Balls

Make these ahead, freeze and enjoy even on a busy morning.

1 lb. bulk sausage, room temperature
1⅓ cup biscuit mix
3 cups grated sharp cheddar cheese

In a medium bowl, mix sausage, biscuit mix and cheese using hands to knead until ingredients are combined. Shape into walnut-sized balls. Place on an ungreased cookie sheet and bake at 400° for 12 to 14 minutes.

Do Ahead Tip: Sausage Balls can be frozen unbaked. Flash freeze them on a cookie sheet. When frozen, place in freezer bags. When ready to serve, bake frozen Sausage Balls for 18 to 20 minutes. Serve hot.

Beef Hash Baskets with Eggs

This easy and tasty dish also makes a nice Sunday supper.

1 can beef hash
6 eggs
¼ cup milk or cream

1 tbs. butter
salt and pepper

Divide hash among 6 lightly greased custard cups. Press to form "baskets." Break an egg into the center of each basket. Dot with butter and cover with 1 tbs. of milk or cream. Add salt and pepper. Bake in a 375° oven for 20 minutes, or until egg is set.

Variations:
- Sprinkle each with 1 tsp. grated Parmesan cheese.
- Sprinkle each with 1 tbs. shredded Swiss, cheddar or Jack cheese.
- Sprinkle each with seasoned bread crumbs.
- Top each with salsa, sour cream and chopped onions after baking.
- Press hash into a greased 8" x 8" pan. Make indentations for eggs and bake as above.
- Substitute corned beef hash for beef hash.

Sausage Pineapple Kabobs

Servings: 4-5

You'll do these again and again. Yum!

1 (10 ozs.) pkg. maple flavored brown-and-serve sausages
1 (20 ozs.) can pineapple chunks, drained
10 small mushrooms
2 tbs. butter, melted
maple syrup

On a wooden skewer, alternate cubes of sausage, pineapple chunks and mushrooms, making 10 kabobs. Brush each with melted butter and maple syrup. Broil 5 minutes on each side.

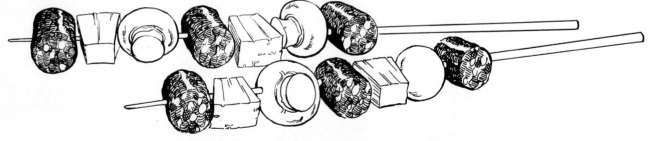

Fruit Compote (page 89), Sausage Pineapple Kabobs (page 136) and Cream Cheese Scrambled Eggs in Toast Cups (page 99) ▶

Apple Sausage

Apples and sausage complement each other in this flavorful dish.

1 pkg. brown-and-serve sausages, cut into chunks
1 large cooking apple, cored and cut into large chunks
1-2 tbs. butter
¼ cup brown sugar
1 tbs. lemon juice

In a medium frying pan, brown sausages and apple in butter. Stir in brown sugar and lemon juice. Heat and serve with eggs, pancakes or waffles.

Variation:
• Add ½ tsp. cinnamon with brown sugar and lemon juice.

Cranberry Sausage

Really delicious. If you cut the sausage into small pieces, it makes a wonderful appetizer eaten with toothpicks.

1 (12 ozs.) pkg. brown-and-serve sausages
1½ tsp. cornstarch
1 tbs. cold water
1 (16 ozs.) can cranberry sauce
¼ tsp. salt
½ tsp. dry mustard
1 tbs. vinegar
½ cup light raisins

In a medium skillet, brown sausage links. Drain any fat. In a small bowl, dissolve cornstarch in water and stir in cranberry sauce. Add salt, mustard and vinegar. Pour over sausages and simmer uncovered for 8 to 10 minutes. Add raisins and continue to simmer for 5 minutes.

French Toast, Pancakes and Waffles

One of these breakfast favorites is a must with many morning diners, and a book on breakfast isn't complete without a substantial section of French toast, pancake and waffle recipes.

Puffy French toast with a sprinkling of powdered sugar or warm maple syrup is a childhood memory I cherish. To me it was a treat even though my efficient mother was just finding a good use for day-old French or Italian bread. Isn't it nice that something so economical is so delicious! You'll find tempting variations here.

The pancakes in this section range from basic Buttermilk Pancakes to the glorious but simple to make Puff Pancake.

And finally, waffles. These soft but crisp cakes can be served with a variety of syrups, sauces and toppings (pages 163-172) or topped with creamed chicken, turkey or tuna for a hearty meal. Or enjoy for dessert, topped with frozen yogurt or ice cream and a sauce.

French Toast, Pancakes and Waffles

French Toast Tips

- Just for fun, make French toast in a waffle iron.

- Cut bread slices in half diagonally.

- Cut each bread slice into several strips.

- Cut bread with cookie cutters for variety.

- To freeze, once bread has absorbed all of egg mixture, place pieces in a single layer on a cookie sheet and freeze until solid. Wrap pieces individually and return to freezer. To serve, place on a lightly greased cookie sheet and bake in a 500° oven for 5 minutes on each side. Brush with melted butter before baking if desired.

- Try different breads for a flavorful variety: challah bread, egg bread, raisin bread, French bread, Italian bread, whole wheat bread, oat bread, granola bread, or rye bread.

Buttermilk French Toast

Buttermilk makes this toast light and fluffy.

2 eggs
1 cup buttermilk
1 tsp. sugar
⅛ tsp. salt
6-8 slices of firm bread
butter or margarine

In a shallow bowl, combine eggs, buttermilk, salt and sugar. Dip bread slices into egg mixture. Coat both sides well. Melt butter or margarine in a large skillet and brown on each side. Serve with syrup, honey or cinnamon and sugar.

Variations:

- **Hawaiian French Toast.** For a taste of Hawaii, substitute ½ cup pineapple juice for milk. Serve with sliced bananas, toasted coconut and powdered sugar.
- **Honey Spice French Toast.** Add 1 tsp. cinnamon and 3 tbs. honey to egg and milk mixture. Serve with cinnamon and sugar.
- **Orange French Toast.** Substitute orange juice for milk and add 1 tsp. grated orange peel. Serve with powdered sugar.
- **Sesame French Toast.** Before turning bread in pan, sprinkle sesame seeds on each piece. Turn and fry until golden brown. Serve seed side up.
- **Nutty French Toast.** Before turning, sprinkle finely chopped nuts on each piece. Turn and serve nut side up.
- **Royal French Toast.** Layer 2-3 pieces of cooked French toast, fresh or frozen sliced peaches or sliced strawberries, sour cream or cottage cheese, nuts and powdered sugar.

English Muffin French Toast

Prepare this easy recipe and freeze some for a quick morning treat.

3 eggs
½ cup milk
4 English muffins, split in half
1 tsp. vanilla
½ tsp. cinnamon

In a 9" x 13" glass dish, mix eggs, milk, vanilla and cinnamon. Place English muffin halves in egg mixture and allow to stand until all of egg mixture is absorbed, about 30 minutes. Fry in butter immediately or cover with plastic wrap and refrigerate overnight. Or to freeze, place muffins on a cookie sheet and freeze uncovered for 1 to 2 hours or until firm. Place in a freezer bag and keep frozen until ready to use. To serve, toast in a toaster until hot or place on a cookie sheet in a 500° oven for 8 to 10 minutes or until golden. Serve with butter and honey.

Eggnog French Toast

Rich and delicious, this is a wonderful holiday treat.

2 cups prepared eggnog
10-12 thick slices of firm bread
butter or margarine

Pour eggnog into a shallow bowl. Dip pieces of bread into eggnog, coating both sides well. Melt butter or margarine in a skillet. Add bread and cook until golden brown on both sides. Serve with powdered sugar or syrup.

Oven Baked French Toast

Servings: 4

No one has to wait long for this cook-all-at-once French toast. You can prepare enough for 4 people all at once.

4 eggs
1 cup evaporated milk
1 tsp. vanilla extract
½ tsp. ground nutmeg
2 tsp. sugar
8 slices of firm bread

In a shallow bowl, beat eggs, milk, vanilla and sugar. Dip bread into mixture until both sides are well coated. Arrange on a lightly greased cookie sheet and bake in a 500° oven for 8 to 10 minutes or until golden brown.

Pancake Tips

- Stir batter just until blended. Don't overmix.
- Test griddle by sprinkling a few drops of water on surface. If the water bounces on the surface, the griddle is ready.
- Pour batter by spoonfuls onto griddle; bake until bubbles appear on the surface, 2 to 3 minutes. Then turn and cook until underside is golden.
- Turn pancakes only once.
- If batter is too thick, thin with milk, juice or water.
- If batter is too thin, add flour, 1 tablespoon at a time.
- Pancakes are best served immediately.
- To freeze, place on a cookie sheet until frozen. Then wrap well and return to freezer. Reheat in toaster, microwave or oven.
- Use any prepared mix to save time. Many variations can be added.
- **Pan-San.** Create a great breakfast sandwich, layering a pancake, egg, pancake, bacon or sausage and another pancake. You may choose to top with butter and syrup.

Do-Ahead Tip: Mix dry ingredients together the night before. Cover. Add liquid ingredients when ready to cook.

Basic Pancake Recipe

With this master recipe, there is no end to the pancake varieties you can create.

2 cups flour
1 tsp. baking powder
½-1 tsp. salt
2-3 tbs. sugar
2 eggs
2 tbs. butter or margarine, melted
1½ cups sour milk or buttermilk

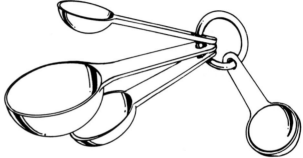

In a medium bowl, mix flour, baking powder, salt and sugar. In a small bowl, beat eggs, milk and butter or margarine. Add to flour mixture. Allow to stand about 5 minutes. Pour by spoonfuls onto hot lightly greased skillet or griddle. Cook until bubbles break on top. Turn and cook until underside is golden.

Variations:

- **Apple Pancakes.** Add 1 cup finely chopped, peeled apple.
- **Bacon Pancakes.** Add ¾ cup cooked, drained and crumbled bacon.
- **Banana Pancakes.** Add 1 large or 2 small chopped bananas.
- **Blueberry Pancakes.** Add 1 cup fresh or frozen blueberries.
- **Chocolate Pancakes.** Increase sugar to ⅓ cup and add 1 square melted unsweetened chocolate.
- **Nut Pancakes.** Add ¼ cup chopped peanuts, pecans, walnuts or filberts.
- **Pineapple Pancakes.** Add 1 cup crushed pineapple, well drained.
- **Whole Wheat Pancakes.** Substitute 1 cup whole wheat flour for 1 cup white flour.

Oven Puff Pancake

A spectacular dish for a family breakfast or to delight weekend guests. Powdered sugar and lemon juice are my favorite accompaniment, but some prefer syrup.

⅓ - ½ cup butter
5 eggs
1¼ cups milk
1 tsp. vanilla

1¼ cups flour
1 tsp. cinnamon
1 tbs. sugar

Melt butter in a 9" x 13" glass dish or in two 9" pie plates in a 425° oven. Meanwhile, in a medium bowl, mix eggs, flour and milk with a wire whisk. Or use a blender or food processor. When butter is melted and sizzling, add batter all at once and bake until puffy and golden brown, 20 to 25 minutes. Serve immediately with powdered sugar and lemon juice or with syrup. Or try a topping (pages 167-172).

Variation:
- **Apple Raisin Puff.** Add 2 cups (about 3 medium) apples, peeled and sliced, ¼ cup white raisins and ¼ cup chopped nuts to heated butter. Return to oven for 2 minutes. Watch carefully so butter doesn't burn. Remove, add batter and proceed as above.

Cottage Cheese Pancakes

25 pancakes

These are delicious with sour cream and sliced sweetened strawberries.

1 cup cottage cheese
2 tbs. melted butter
4 eggs
1 tsp. sugar
½ tsp. baking powder
½ cup sifted flour
1 tsp. sugar
¼ tsp. salt

Mix cottage cheese in a blender or food processor until smooth. Add eggs and melted butter and blend a few seconds. Add flour, sugar and salt and blend again. Drop batter by tablespoons onto hot griddle or pan. Shape with back of spoon. Turn when underside is light brown.

Hawaiian French Toast (page 145) ▶

Waffle Tips

- Pour batter from a pitcher.

- Pour batter in the center of the waffle iron grid.

- Fill grid only ⅔ full. Do not overfill or batter will overflow.

- Test heated waffle iron by sprinkling it with a few drops of water. When water bounces on surface, the heat is perfect.

- Most waffles take 3-5 minutes to bake.

- For crisper waffles, leave waffle in iron a minute or so after it stops steaming.

- To freeze waffles, cool waffles completely on a wire rack after baking. Wrap each waffle separately in plastic wrap. Then place all in a plastic bag. Or place cooled waffles on a cookie sheet, freeze until firm and wrap well in plastic or foil.

- Reheat frozen waffles in a toaster or in a 425° oven for 4-5 minutes. Or use a microwave.

- Make a waffle sandwich with almost any filling.

◀ Waffles (page 158), Orange Butter, Strawberry Butter and Honey Nut Butter (page 162)

Waffles

Crisp on the outside, soft on the inside and light as air.

2 cups sifted flour
3 tsp. baking powder
2 tbs. sugar
1 tsp. salt
3 egg yolks, beaten
3 egg whites, beaten until stiff
1¼ cups milk
4 tbs. butter or margarine, melted

In a medium bowl, sift flour, baking powder, sugar and salt. In a small bowl, mix beaten egg yolks, milk and shortening. Add to dry ingredients, stirring lightly until mixed. Bake in a hot waffle iron.

Sprinkle-Over-Batter Variations:
- 2 tbs. coarsely chopped nuts
- fresh or thawed frozen blueberries

- raisins or chopped dried fruit
- grated semisweet chocolate
- thinly sliced banana
- finely chopped ham
- cooked, sliced sausage links
- cooked, crumbled bulk sausage

Add-To-Batter Variations:

- **Apple Waffles.** Add 1 tsp. cinnamon with dry ingredients. Add 1 cup chopped, peeled apple to batter. Serve with warm applesauce and sour cream. Or serve with Orange Maple Syrup (page 164).
- **Blueberry Waffles.** Add 1 cup fresh or frozen blueberries, thawed and drained, to dry ingredients.
- **Chocolate Waffles.** Add ½ cup cocoa and an additional ¼ cup sugar to dry ingredients. Serve with whipped cream and nuts.
- **Orange Waffles.** Add 1 tbs. grated orange rind to batter and substitute ½ cup orange juice for ½ cup milk. Serve with Creamy Orange Topping (page 172).
- **Spice Waffles.** Add 1 tsp. cinnamon and ½ tsp. nutmeg to dry ingredients. Add 3 tbs. molasses to liquid ingredients.

Sour Cream Waffles

These wonderful light waffles are unbelievably tender.

1½ cups flour
2 tsp. sugar
½ tsp. baking soda
1 tsp. baking powder
½ tsp. salt
3 eggs
2 cups (1 pint) sour cream
¼ cup butter, melted

In a medium bowl, sift flour, sugar, soda, baking powder and salt. In another bowl, beat eggs until light and frothy. Blend in sour cream. Add dry ingredients and mix well. Blend in melted butter. Bake in a hot waffle iron.

Do-Ahead Tip: This batter will keep, covered, in the refrigerator for 3 days.

Butters, Syrups, Sauces and Toppings

Dress any breakfast in style with the recipes in this section. Sweet flavored butters are the perfect accompaniment for breakfast muffins, breads, waffles, pancakes, French toast or to glorify even plain toast.

The syrups, sauces and toppings are the delicious finishing touch to pancakes, waffles and French toast as well as to fruits and custards.

Butters

These delicious butters are so quick you can whip them up in minutes and keep them in the refrigerator to be enjoyed anytime.

- Use unsalted butter at room temperature for best results.
- Blend butter using a wire whisk, blender or processor.
- Store in a tightly covered container in the refrigerator.
- To ¼ lb. butter at room temperature, add any of the following:

Cranberry Butter . . . add
2 tbs. honey
2 tbs. finely chopped fresh cranberries

Orange Butter . . . add
1 tbs. orange peel
2 tbs. orange juice concentrate
4 tbs. powdered sugar

Jam Butter . . . add
2 tbs. marmalade and ½ tsp. ginger **or**
2 tbs. strawberry, raspberry or
blackberry jam **or** ½ tsp. cinnamon,
⅛ tsp. allspice and 2 tbs. jam

Strawberry Butter . . . add
¼ cup powdered sugar
¼ cup chopped strawberries

Honey Nut Butter . . . add
2 tbs. honey
¼ cup chopped pecans, walnuts
or filberts

Spicy Butter . . . add
1 tsp. cinnamon
2 tbs. honey

Chutney Butter . . . add
2 tbs. chutney

Rum Cinnamon Syrup

A delicious sauce for ice cream, too. Good warm or at room temperature. Because this is a great recipe for gift giving, the second recipe is included to fill six ½-pint jars.

½ cup water
2 cinnamon sticks
1 cup white corn syrup

½ cup brown sugar
⅛ tsp. rum extract

In a small saucepan, place water and cinnamon stick. Bring to a boil, cover and simmer for 15 minutes. Add corn syrup and brown sugar, stirring until dissolved. Bring to a boil again. Remove from heat and stir in rum extract. Serve warm over waffles and pancakes.

1½ cups water
8 inches of stick cinnamon
3 cups white corn syrup

1½ cups brown sugar
¼ tsp. rum extract

Follow directions above. Strain out cinnamon sticks. Pour syrup into six ½-pint sterilized jars.

Orange Maple Syrup

Rich and wonderful when calories don't count!

2 cups maple flavored syrup
1 cup butter

1½ tsp. grated orange peel
2 tsp. orange liqueur

In a small saucepan, heat syrup, butter, orange peel and liqueur for 5 minutes. Serve warm.

Creamy Molasses Syrup

If you like the flavor of molasses, you'll love this.

½ cup molasses
¾ cup evaporated milk
1-3 tbs. butter

In a small saucepan, heat molasses, milk and butter until combined and hot. Serve warm over pancakes and waffles.

Cinnamon Peach Sauce

This is a delicious sauce, especially good served warm.

1 (8¾ ozs.) can sliced peaches, packed in their own juice
orange juice
⅓ cup white or brown sugar
2 tsp. corn starch
¼ tsp. apple pie spice **or** ¼ tsp. ground cinnamon, ⅛ tsp. nutmeg,
⅛ tsp. allspice.

Drain peach juice into 1 cup measure. Add orange juice to make one cup. In a small saucepan, heat mixture to boiling. Combine sugar and cornstarch and stir into boiling mixture. Stir over medium heat until thickened and clear. Add peaches and serve warm or chilled over waffles, pancakes and French toast.

Cherry Maple Waffle Sauce

2½ cups

A sweet and colorful sauce.

1 (16 ozs.) can pitted, dark or light sweet cherries
1 cup maple-flavored syrup

Drain cherries. In a saucepan, combine cherries and maple syrup. Heat just until hot. Do not boil. Serve warm.

Variations:
* Add ¼ tsp. ground allspice.
* Add 1 tsp. lemon juice.
* Add ½ tsp. almond extract.

Creamy Toppings

Make any of these tasty toppings with plain yogurt, sour half-and-half or sour cream.

Mix 1 cup (8 ozs.) of yogurt, sour half-and-half or sour cream with:

- 3 tbs. brown sugar and 1 tsp. nutmeg
- 2 tbs. maple syrup and 1 tsp. grated orange peel
- 3 tbs. applesauce and 1 tbs. cinnamon-sugar
- ¼ cup orange marmalade, jam or preserves
- 3 tbs. drained crushed pineapple, ⅛ tsp. ginger and ½ tsp. cinnamon
- 3 tbs. honey, ½ cup fresh fruit and ¼ cup toasted pecans
- 3 tbs. whole cran-raspberry sauce and ¼ cup toasted pecans

Blend all and heat just to warm, or serve cold over pancakes, waffles or French toast.

Cranberry Topping

4¾ cups

Brandy and cranberries make a wonderful combination.

1 cup sugar
1½ cups water

2 cups cranberries
¼ cup brandy

Mix sugar, water and cranberries together in a medium saucepan. Simmer 7 minutes. Stir in brandy and serve warm.

Orange Honey Topping

1 cup

This topping is always a favorite.

¾ cup honey
¼ cup orange juice concentrate
1 tbs. butter (optional)

⅛ tsp. cloves
¼ tsp. cinnamon

In a small saucepan, heat honey, concentrate and butter. Stir in spices and serve.

Quick Pineapple Topping

Lightly toast almonds for a richly nutty taste.

1 (8 ozs.) can crushed pineapple
1 cup orange marmalade

yogurt, sour half-and-half or sour cream
slivered almonds, toasted

In a small saucepan, mix drained crushed pineapple with marmalade. Heat and serve. Add a dollop of yogurt, sour half-and-half or sour cream and sprinkle with almonds.

Fluffy Cream Cheese Topping

¾ cup

Save orange or lemon peels in a plastic bag in the freezer. It's always ready to grate at a moment's notice.

1 (8 ozs.) pkg. cream cheese, softened
¼ cup powdered sugar

1 tsp. vanilla
1 tsp. grated lemon or orange peel

In a small bowl, beat cream cheese, powdered sugar, vanilla and lemon peel together until light and fluffy.

Cream Cheese Topping

½ cup

Keep some of this easy topping in the refrigerator to serve anytime.

1 (8 ozs.) pkg. cream cheese, softened
3 tbs. honey
3 tbs. chopped pecans

In a small bowl, beat cream cheese and honey. Stir in pecans. Makes ½ cup.

Brandied Cranberries

5 cups

Freeze several bags of fresh cranberries in season and you can enjoy their special flavor all year around. No need to thaw before using.

1 (12 ozs.) bag fresh cranberries
2 cups sugar
1 cup brandy

Pour cranberries into a lightly greased 9" x 13" pan. Mix sugar and brandy and spread over cranberries. Stir to coat well. Cover pan lightly with foil and bake 45 minutes at 300°. Cool and refrigerate. Serve with pancakes, waffles, custard, add to a fruit compote or use to garnish a fresh fruit plate.

Banana Honey Topping

1 cup

A sweet tropical complement to pancakes or waffles. Delicious with muffins, too.

2 ripe bananas
3-4 tbs. honey
2 tbs. softened butter or margarine

Peel and mash bananas well. Stir in honey and butter. Serve immediately.

Strawberry Cream Topping

1 cup

Great spread on pancakes or with fruit.

1 (3 ozs.) pkg. cream cheese, softened
¼ cup sugar
1 cup strawberries, fresh or frozen

½ tsp. lemon extract **or**
2 tsp. cream sherry

In a small bowl, beat cream cheese and sugar until blended. Add strawberries, lemon extract or sherry and beat until well blended. Cover and chill.

Creamy Orange Topping

*Turn this into **Creamy Lemon Topping** by substituting lemonade concentrate for orange and eliminating the sugar.*

1 cup half-and-half
¼ cup partially thawed orange juice concentrate
2 tbs. sugar
2 tsp. orange liqueur **or** almond liqueur **or** vanilla **or** almond extract

In a small bowl, use a wire whisk to beat half-and-half, juice concentrate, sugar and liqueur or extract well. Cover and chill 30 minutes or overnight. Mixture will thicken.

Special Occasion and Holiday Breakfasts

An invitation to breakfast is a friendly, warm way to start the day in a special way. And it's often less expensive to entertain at breakfast. Here are ideas for a variety of breakfast parties for everyone from preschool age children to new people in the neighborhood, from a business breakfast to a bridal shower.

And of course it's great fun to celebrate holidays with a special breakfast. So I've included plenty of fuss-free, do-ahead menus and ideas for holiday breakfasts for family and guests.

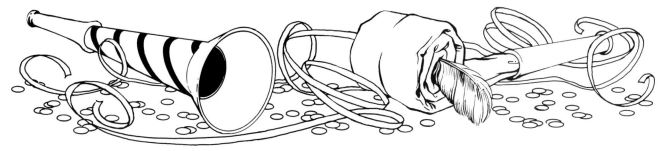

Special Occasion and Holiday Breakfasts

Welcome to the Neighborhood Breakfast

What could be friendlier for a new family in the neighborhood than to be greeted by welcoming neighbors at an informal breakfast? Make pitchers of Orange Juliettes and wine coolers. Guests can join in to make fajitas, a comfortable, informal way to get acquainted. There will be lots of new friendships before this party ends.

Menu
Orange Juliettes (page 16)
Melon wedges filled with berries
Scrambled Eggs Fajitas (page 112)
Albertina's Brown Sugar Muffins (page 54)
Honey Nut Butter (page 162)

Weekend Garden Party Breakfast

This warm weather party idea is a charming way to enjoy a morning meal. Celebrate a birthday, promotion, or just celebrate summer! Potted plants gathered around the eating area offer the perfect decoration and fresh flowers tucked into small flower pots make charming centerpieces.

Menu
Fresh fruit
Lemon Yogurt Fruit Dip (page 94)
Sausage Strata (page 106)
Granola Muffins (page 50)
Spicy Butter (page 162)

Club Meeting or Business Breakfast

This is a relatively new idea in meeting styles that is gaining popularity. Everyone is fresh and ready to get to work and gathering for an informal morning meal is a friendly and nonthreatening atmosphere. Pitchers of juices, fresh fruit compote and a variety of muffins make this a simple to prepare, help yourself kind of meal.

Menu
Tangy Citrus Cooler (page 15)
Apricot Cooler (page 14)
Orange juice
Fruit Compote (page 89)
Granola Muffins (page 50)
Refrigerator Bran Muffins (page 46)

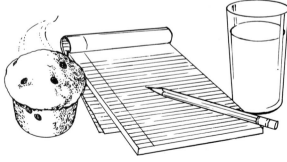

Before School Birthday Breakfast

When a child's birthday falls on a school day, why not start the day with a simple morning celebration? Ask friends to come just for an hour. A nutritious, low sugar breakfast helps the children get ready for the school day. Party hats and novelty pencils, erasers and paper make appropriate favors that can be used at school.

Menu
Orange Juliette (page 16)
Fruit Kabobs (page 81)
Twice Baked Potatoes with
    Egg and Cheese (page 128)

Sweet Sixteen Slumber Party Breakfast

Delight a gaggle of girls with this great help yourself breakfast. Freeze different variations of waffles ahead of time, and reheat them in the oven in the morning. Arrange containers of butters, syrups, sauces and toppings for everyone to help herself. Serve sparkling juices in stemmed glasses for a special look.

Menu
Waffles and variations (page 158)
Butters, Syrups, Sauces and Toppings (page 161)
Cranberry Spritz and sparkling juices (page 18)
Do-Ahead Sausages (page 133)

After the Run or Parade Breakfast

Celebrate even if you came in last! You made it! Or invite everyone to your house after a Saturday morning club or church activity.

Menu
Juices
Fruit Kabobs (page 81)
Granola Muffins (page 50)

Summer Picnic Breakfast

This packable menu is simple to serve and to eat. A small bouquet of flowers, a fuss-free tablecloth and terry cloth fingertip towel napkins with silverware wrapped inside can turn this into a delightful outdoor meal.

Menu
Sparkling juices (page 18)
Fresh fruit
Egg Roll Quiche (page 114)
Blueberry Cinnamon Muffins (page 56)

Bridal Shower Breakfast

Breakfast is a wonderful time for a shower. Cover the table with a lace tablecloth and gather each corner up with a big bow, letting the ribbons trail for a festively feminine look. Fill baskets with small potted flowers for a centerpiece and send each guest happily home with a pot of flowers as a favor.

Menu
Curried Fruit (page 91)
Brunch Puffs (page 108)
Best-Ever Banana Bread (page 32)
Spicy Butter (page 162)

Baby Shower Breakfast

Tie small baby items and bows onto a small potted bush or even a tiny tree to use as a pretty centerpiece. Then send it all home with the mother-to-be as your gift. Multiply the menu for a large crowd.

Menu
Strawberry Supreme (page 87)
Sausage Strata (page 106)
Albertina's Brown Sugar Muffins (page 54)

Fall Tailgate Breakfast

What a glorious way to enjoy the palate of gold fall hues. Or use this menu for a before-the-game tailgate party. You might even want to enjoy this idea later in the season for a Christmas tree cutting expedition.

Menu
Hot Chocolate (page 21)
Hot Apple Toddy (page 24)
Quick Cinnamon Rolls (page 40)
Strawberry Butter (page 162)

Breakfast Gift Baskets

Create a celebration breakfast basket for a welcome birthday, anniversary, new mother, new home, happy promotion or simply to say congratulations. Include muffins or bread, hot chocolate mixes and overnight compote and maybe a bottle of sparkling cider or champagne. Use a pretty square of cloth cut with pinking shears or use a tea towel or napkin to line the basket. Festive paper napkins, a few fresh flowers and a balloon tied to the basket handle all say, "You are special. Have a happy day!"

New Year's Eve Midnight Breakfast

Create a party mood using any leftover star decorations from the holidays. Use red and white candles and add black to the color scheme for a touch of sophistication. Place groupings of candles on square mirror tiles (found in most home improvement departments). Surround with gold ribbons and tuck in stars. Invite friends over to ring in the New Year with a casual breakfast where guests participate in the cooking. With all the ingredients prepared ahead of time, made-to-order omelets are filled to please each guest. Have plenty of coffee, but be sure to offer a decaffeinated one and herb teas as well.

Menu
Champagne or sparkling juices (page 18)
Fruit Compote (page 89)
Omelets with various fillings (page 104)
Muffin varieties (pages 44 to 56)

New Year's Day Brunch

In some countries, it is a tradition to have company on New Year's Day because it brings good fortune throughout the year. Have a Mexican breakfast for friends and neighbors, and let everyone create his own fajita. Bring out the solid colored cloth and napkins in red, yellow or blue, serve items in pottery or terra cotta bowls and add a basket of brightly colored paper flowers.

Menu
Wine coolers
Fresh fruit plate
Scrambled Eggs Fajitas (page 112)
  or
Fantastic Mexican Egg Dish (page 121)
Best-Ever Banana Bread (page 32)
Orange Cranberry Bread (page 33)

Valentine Breakfast

Treat sweethearts to a glorious pink and white breakfast. Sprinkle a white tablecloth with red paper hearts and bring out red, pink, or white items for decorations. Tie glasses and napkins with tiny red bows to add to the festive mood. Delight your family and friends with this easy menu that says, "I love you!"

Menu
Mint Hot Chocolate (page 21)
Rosy Cinnamon Applesauce (page 85)
Waffles with strawberries and whipped cream
    (page 158)

St. Patrick's Day Breakfast

Everyone is Irish on this day, so celebrate with a Top o' the Mornin' menu. Add a shamrock plant to the table and run green ribbons down the center for that extra touch of Ireland.

Menu
Tea and Coffee
Grapes Delight (page 87)
Irish Tea Bread (page 36)
Basic Buttermilk Biscuits (page 26)
Currant Scones (page 34)

Easter Breakfast

Fill an excelsior-lined basket with eggs and tuck in flowers for a spring-fresh centerpiece. Use an egg with a guest's name on it, placed in a tiny basket, for each placecard. Most of the menu can be prepared the night before. Mix the juices for the Apricot Cooler and refrigerate in a large pitcher; add soda just before serving. Mix the Fruit Compote the night before. Bake the puffs and mix the filling, then fill and bake in the morning. Of course the muffins can be baked in the morning from batter you've kept in the refrigerator.

Menu
Apricot Cooler (page 14)
Fruit Compote (page 89)
Brunch Puffs (page 108)
Refrigerator Bran Muffins (page 46)
Strawberry Butter (page 162)

Mother's Day Breakfast

Honor Mom with a meal fit for a queen. And this menu is so easy even children can create it. For a really special treat serve her breakfast in bed. Add a bouquet of flowers and a handmade card from the children and watch Mom glow. Then show her how special she is with a coupon book filled with promises of things you'll do for her whenever she desires.

Menu
Grapes Delight (page 87)
Quick Quiche (page 122)
Jan's Popovers (page 58)

Father's Day Breakfast

Here's another royal menu just for Dad. Even if you've never made Hollandaise sauce before, this one is foolproof. Best of all, the entire menu can be done ahead with special tips, and you'll have more time to spend with Dad.

Menu
Fresh fruit with Lemon Yogurt Fruit Dip (page 94)
Eggs Benedict in Puff Pastry (page 116)
Cinnamon Pull-Apart (page 31)

Fourth of July Breakfast

Here's a star-spangled morning party. Pull out anything red, white and blue to carry out the holiday theme. Tuck little toothpick flags into buffet items. Prepare batters ahead and use several waffle irons and grills if possible, depending on the size of the crowd. Let each guest prepare his own waffle to order. Make sauces or simply arrange bowls of sliced strawberries and blueberries with whipped cream or sour cream and toppings. It's a casual, fun way to celebrate America!

Menu
Sparkling juices (page 18)
Fresh fruit plate
Pancakes (page 150)
Sour Cream Waffles (page 160)
Cherry Maple Waffle Sauce (page 166)
Strawberry Cream Topping (page 171)
Whipped cream and sour cream
Nuts, coconut and chocolate shavings

Mother's Back to School Breakfast

After a long summer with the kids, a group of moms in our neighborhood get together for a visit over breakfast on the first day of school. It's a fun way to begin the new school year. There always seems to be plenty of fresh zucchini in September so the Zucchini Frittata makes the perfect light main dish, accompanied by sliced fresh melons and muffins.

Menu
Sliced fresh melon
Zucchini Frittata (page 103)
Granola Muffins (page 50)
Orange Butter (page 162)

Fall Breakfast

Gather beautiful harvest vegetables and arrange a centerpiece. Or use a pumpkin as a vase and fill it with fall flowers. Cut a hole in the center of several beautifully shined apples and fit in candles for harvest candle holders. Golden fall colors or orange, rust and brown are the perfect accompaniment to this celebration of the season.

Menu
Quick Cinnamon Cider (page 24)
Apricot Cooler (page 14)
Corn Muffin Pie (page 57)

Thanksgiving Breakfast

Families and friends often have to divide their time on Thanksgiving to see everyone. Why not have a morning gathering to enjoy those people you might otherwise not get to see? Keep the menu light, since there is a big meal ahead. Or you might have a breakfast gathering the day after Thanksgiving. Of course the Golden Turkey Bread is a show-stopping addition to this occasion.

Menu
Curried Fruit (page 91)
Golden Turkey Bread (page 42)
Refrigerator Bran Muffins (page 46)
Cranberry Butter (page 162)

Christmas Breakfast

You'll have plenty of time to enjoy opening presents on Christmas morning with this easy and delicious do-ahead breakfast. Make the Christmas Tree Bread ahead of time and freeze. Heat and frost just before serving. For a heartier menu add a Sausage Puff that you have put together several days ahead and popped into the oven Christmas morning. Even the Fruit Compote is do-ahead: add the bananas and serve. Why not spread out a blanket and have a winter picnic in front of the tree?

Menu
Hot Chocolate (page 21)
Fruit Compote (page 89)
Christmas Tree Bread (page 42)
Sausage Puff (page 107)

Index

METRIC CONVERSION CHART

Liquid or Dry Measuring Cup (based on an 8 ounce cup)
1/4 cup = 60 ml
1/3 cup = 80 ml
1/2 cup = 125 ml
3/4 cup = 190 ml
1 cup = 250 ml
2 cups = 500 ml

Liquid or Dry Measuring Cup (based on a 10 ounce cup)
1/4 cup = 80 ml
1/3 cup = 100 ml
1/2 cup = 150 ml
3/4 cup = 230 ml
1 cup = 300 ml
2 cups = 600 ml

Liquid or Dry Teaspoon and Tablespoon
1/4 tsp. = 1.5 ml
1/2 tsp. = 3 ml
1 tsp. = 5 ml
3 tsp. = 1 tbs. = 15 ml

Temperatures

°F		°C
200	=	100
250	=	120
275	=	140
300	=	150
325	=	160
350	=	180
375	=	190
400	=	200
425	=	220
450	=	230
475	=	240
500	=	260
550	=	280

Pan Sizes (1 inch = 25mm)
8-inch pan (round or square) = 200 mm x 200 mm
9-inch pan (round or square) = 225 mm x 225 mm
9 x 5 x 3-inch loaf pan = 225 mm x 125 mm x 75 mm
1/4 inch thickness = 5 mm
1/8 inch thickness = 2.5 mm

Pressure Cooker
100 Kpa = 15 pounds per square inch
70 Kpa = 10 pounds per square inch
35 Kpa = 5 pounds per square inch

Mass
1 ounce = 30 g
4 ounces = 1/4 pound = 125 g
8 ounces = 1/2 pounds = 250 g
16 ounces = 1 pound = 500 g
2 pounds = 1 kg

Key (America uses an 8 ounce cup — Britain uses a 10 ounce cup)

ml = milliliter
l = liter
g = gram
K = Kilo (one thousand)
mm = millimeter
m = mill (a thousandth)
°F = degrees Fahrenheit

°C = degrees Celsius
tsp. = teaspoon
tbs. = tablespoon
Kpa = (pounds pressure per square inch)
    This configuration is used for pressure cookers only.

Metric equivalents are rounded to conform to existing metric measuring utensils.